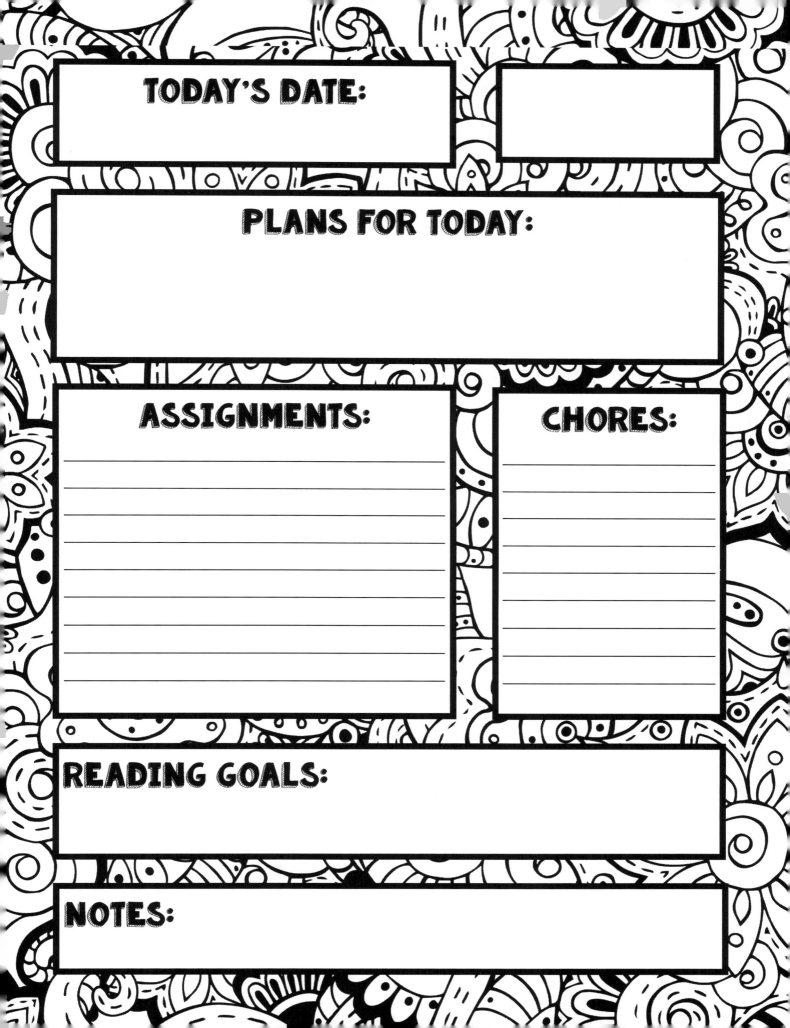

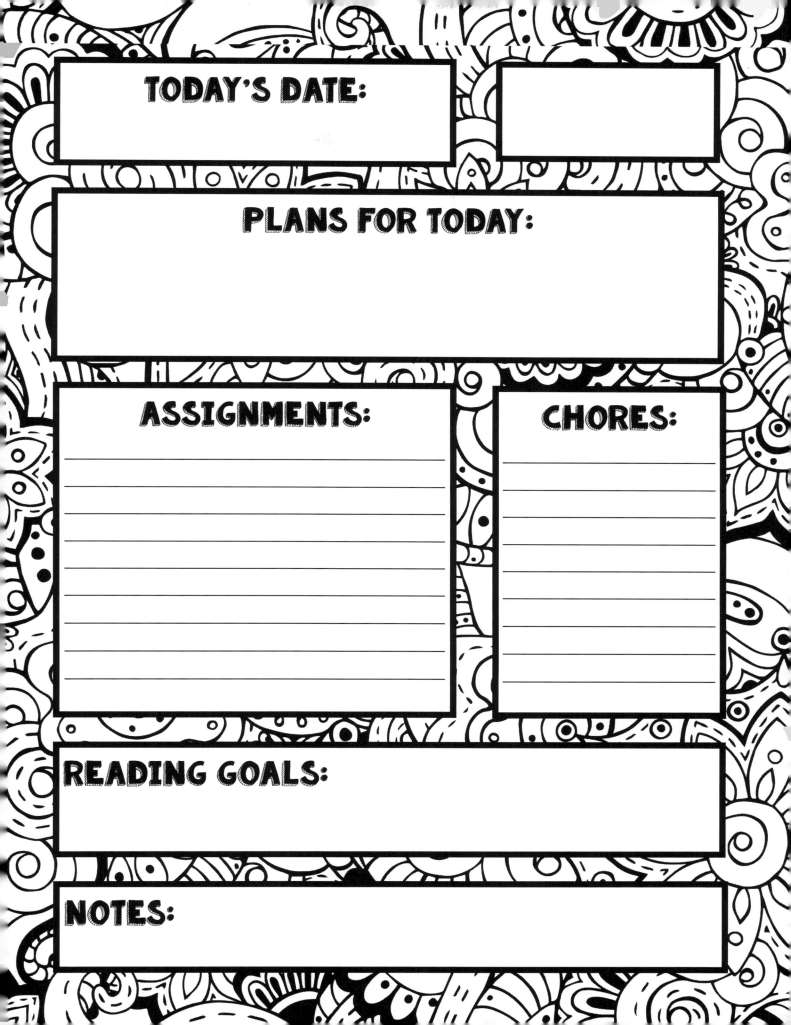

Plans & Perspective

"The home is the first and most effective place to learn the lessons of life: truth, honor, virtue, self control, the value of education, honest work, and the purpose and privilege of life." -McKay

My True Priorities

Long Term Goals

I Am Thankful For...

Checklist

Remember...

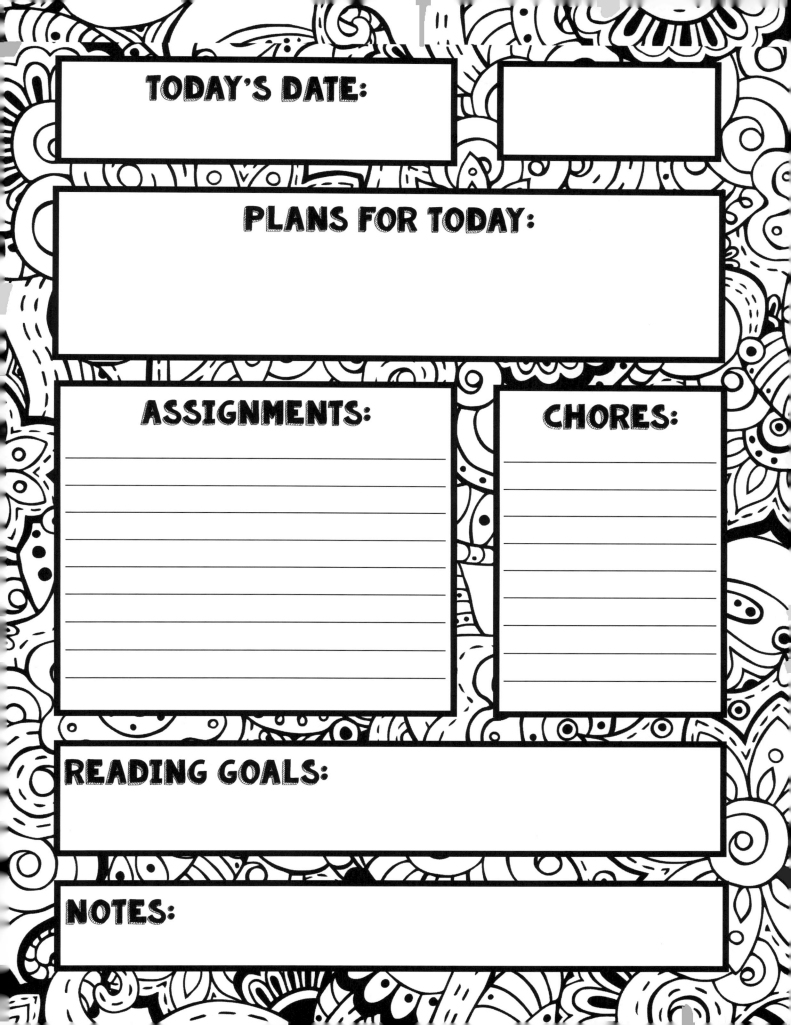

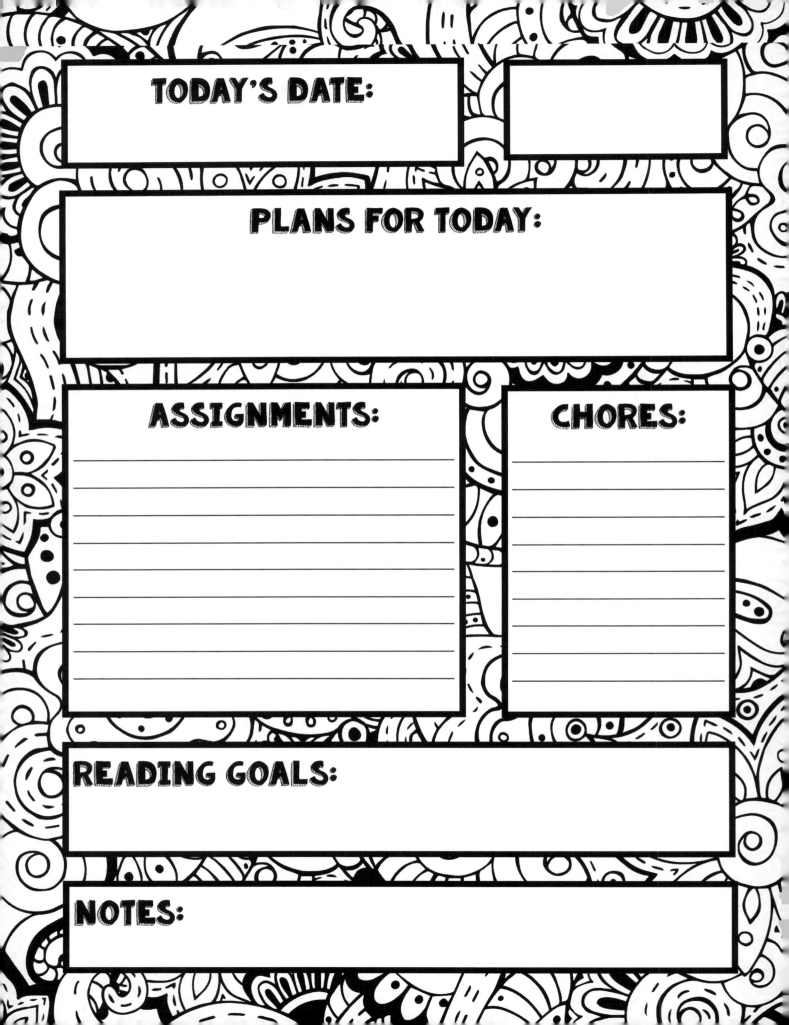

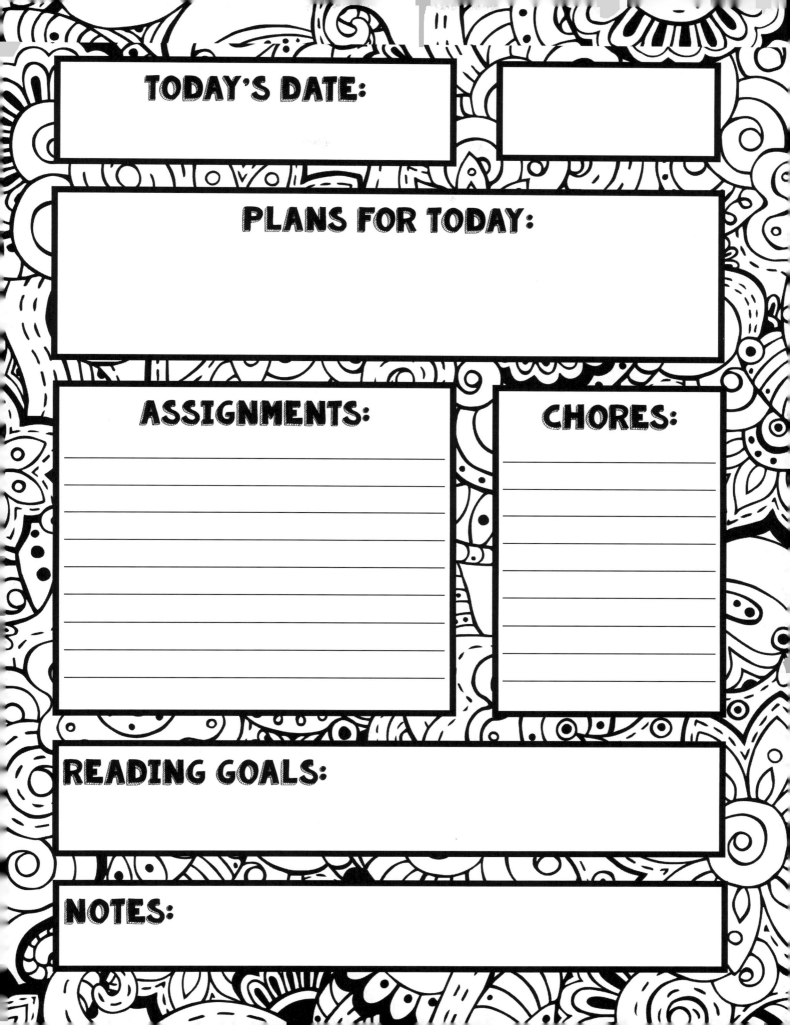

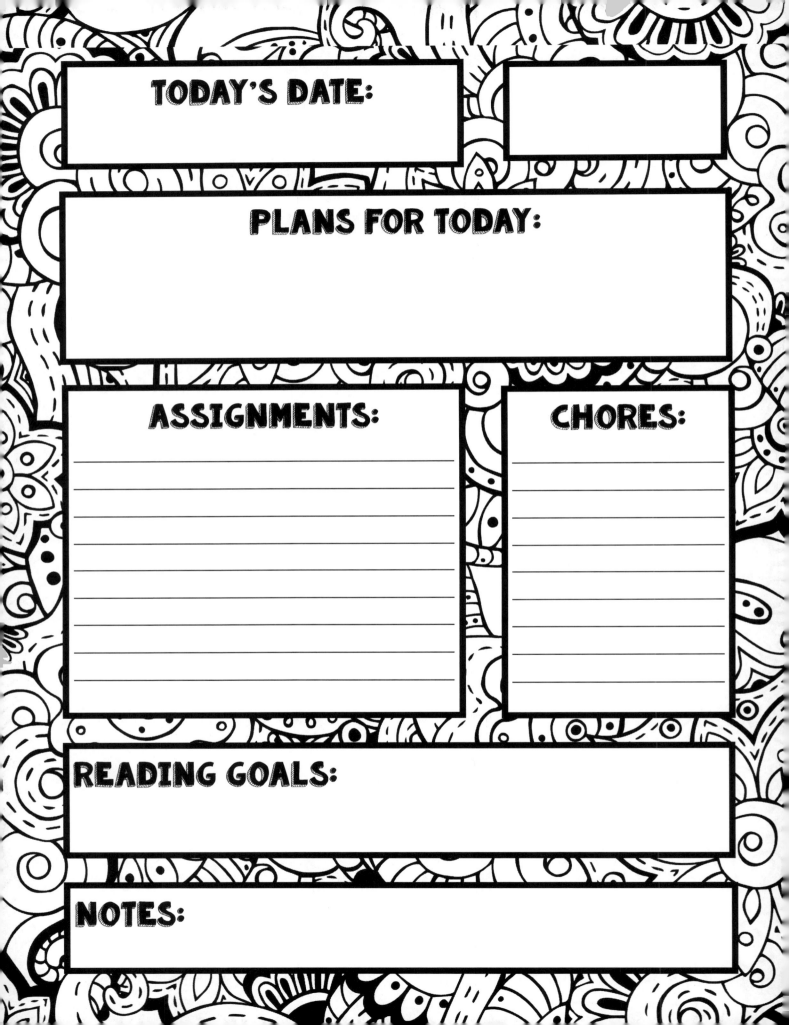

Plans & Perspective

"The home is the first and most effective place to learn the lessons of life: truth, honor, virtue, self control, the value of education, honest work, and the purpose and privilege of life." -McKay

My True Priorities

Long Term Goals

I Am Thankful For...

Checklist

Remember...

_____
_____
_____
_____
_____

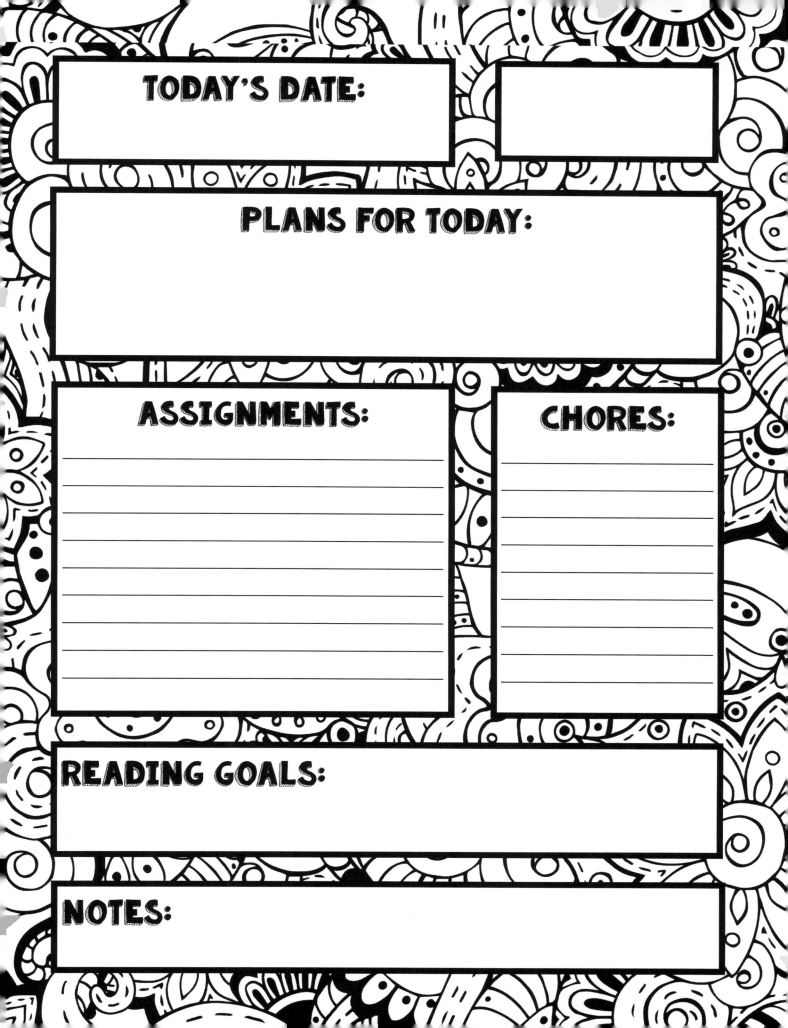

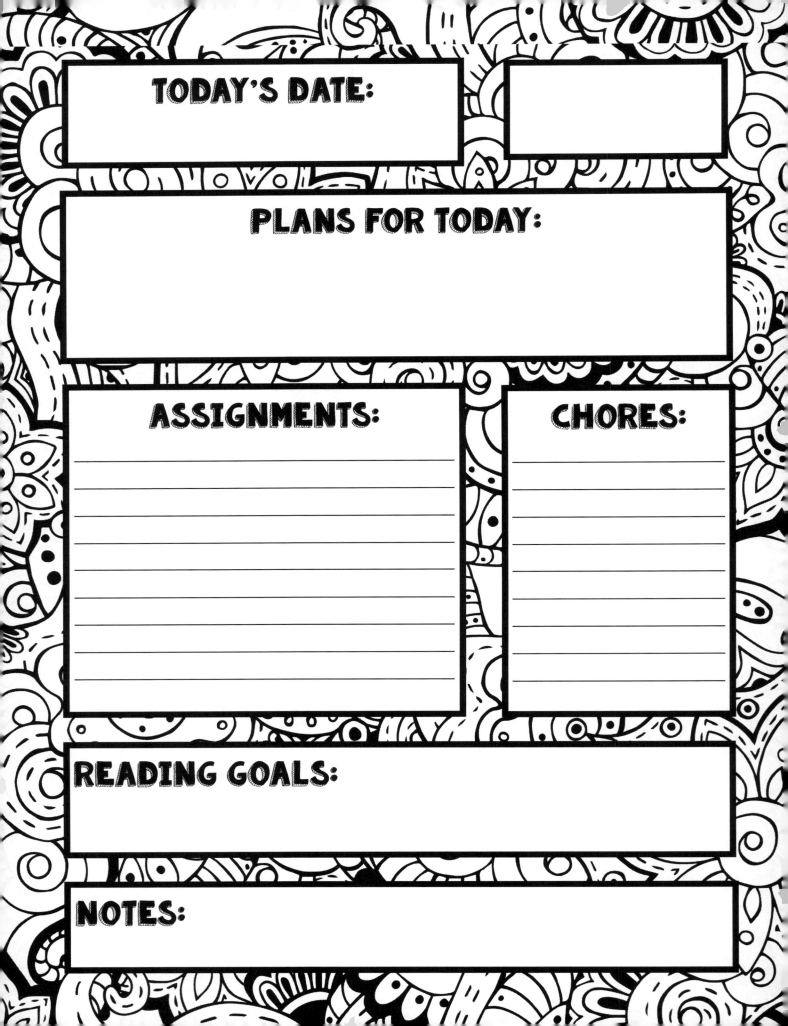

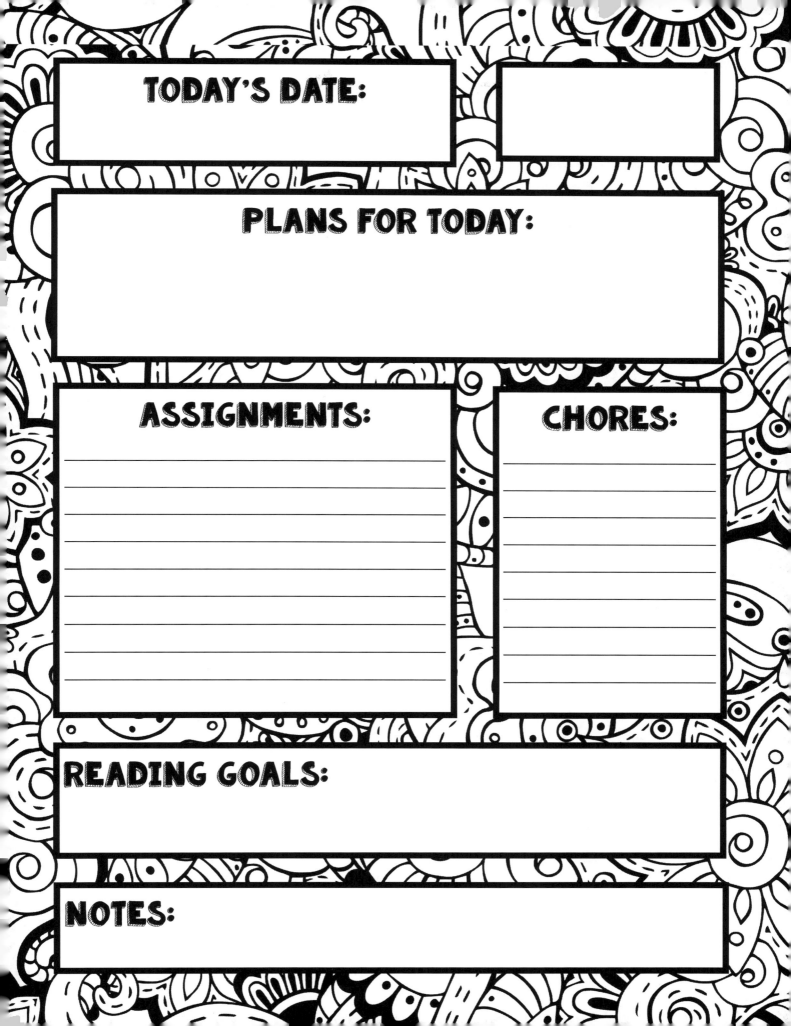

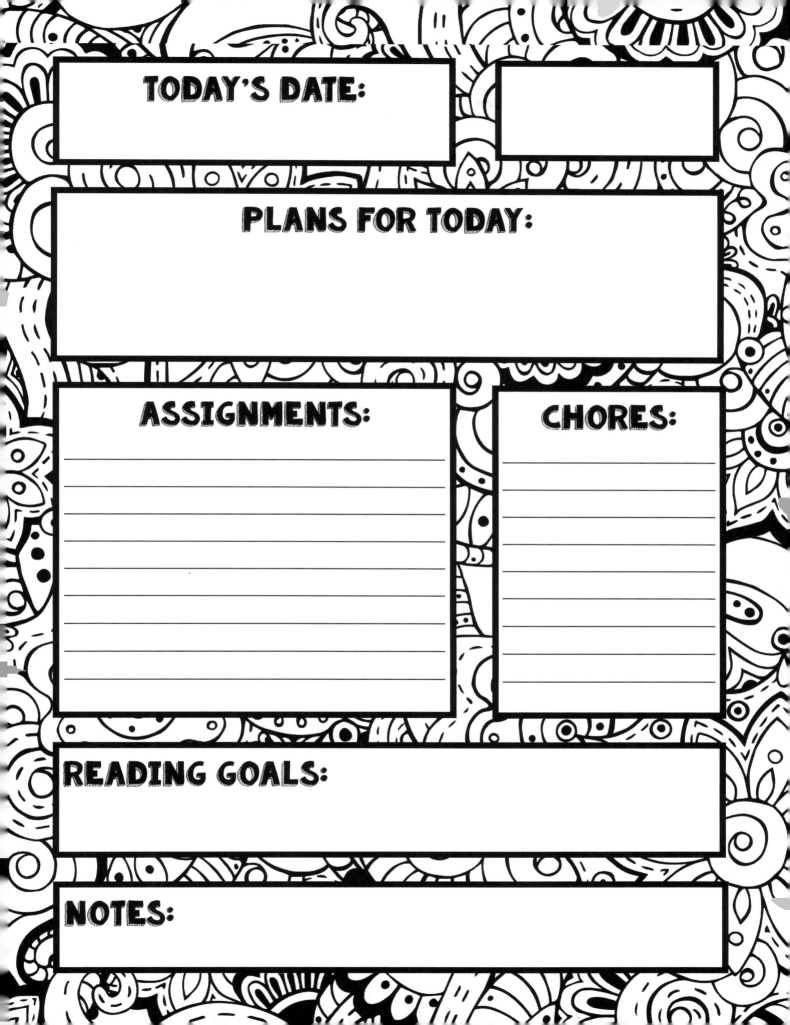

Plans & Perspective

"The home is the first and most effective place to learn the lessons of life: truth, honor, virtue, self control, the value of education, honest work, and the purpose and privilege of life." -McKay

My True Priorities

Long Term Goals

I Am Thankful For...

Checklist

Remember...

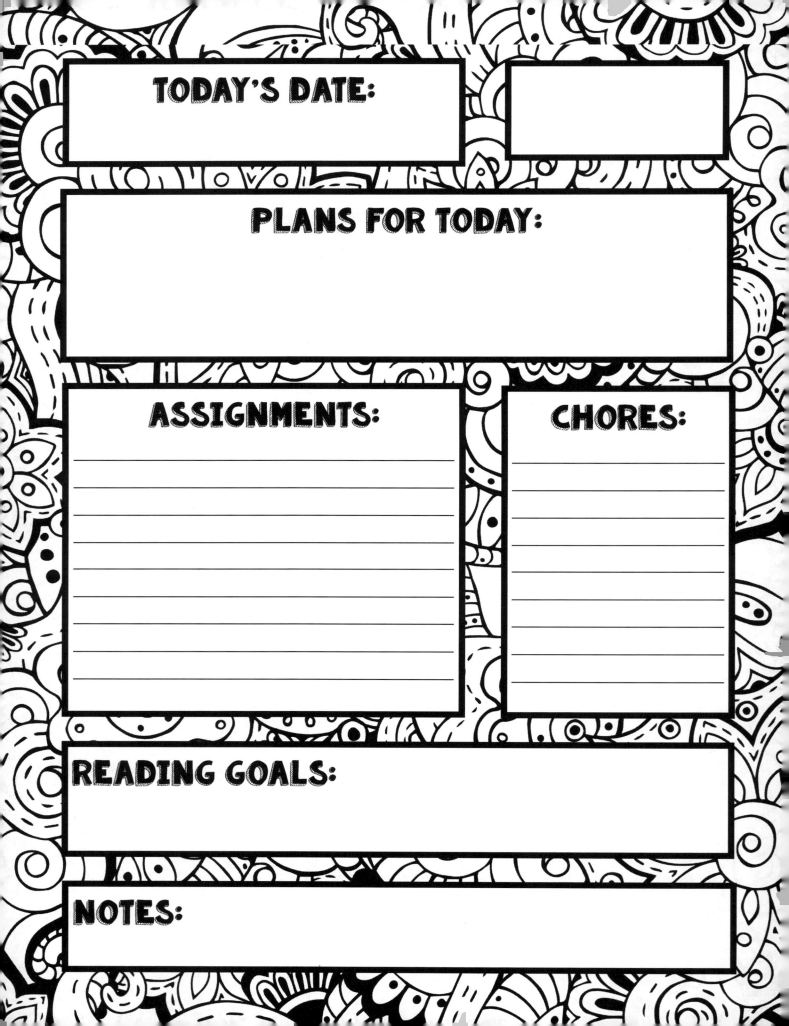

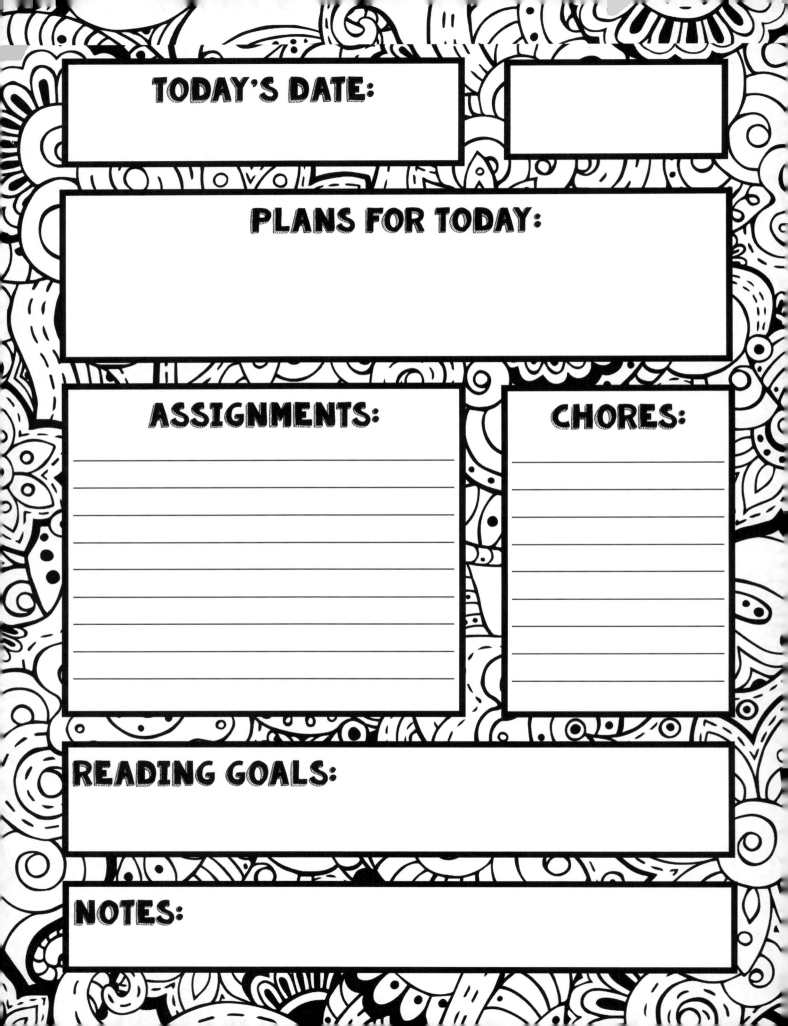

Plans & Perspective

"The home is the first and most effective place to learn the lessons of life: truth, honor, virtue, self control, the value of education, honest work, and the purpose and privilege of life." -McKay

My True Priorities

Long Term Goals

I Am Thankful For...

Checklist

Remember...

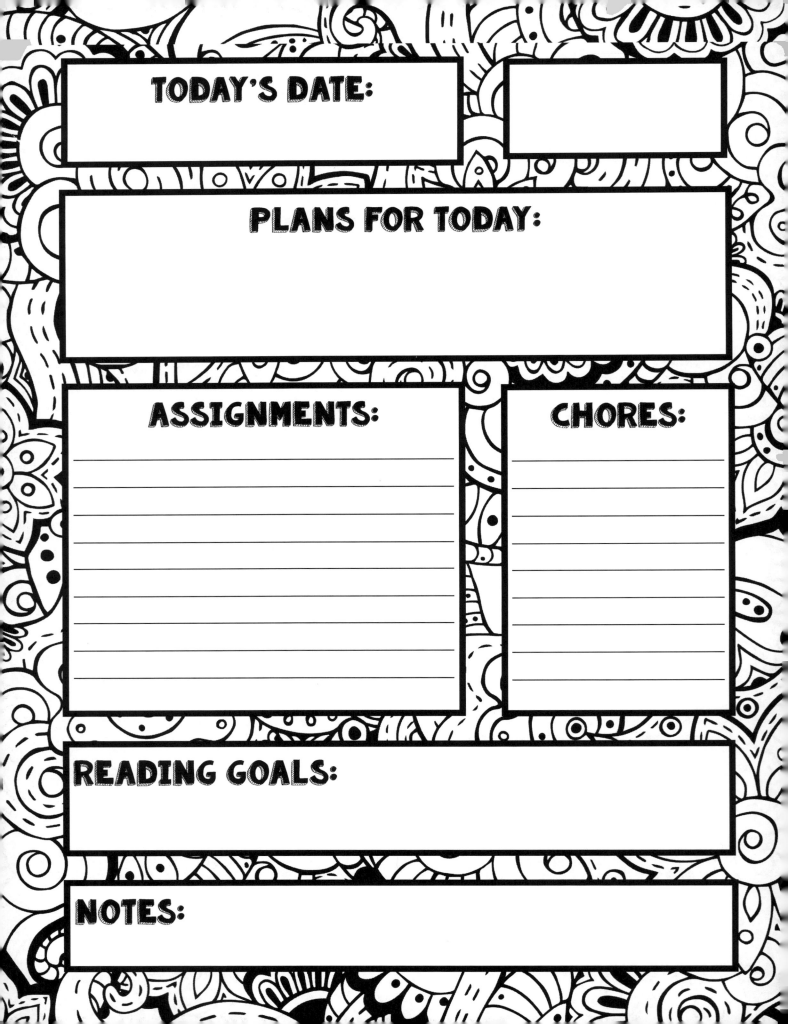

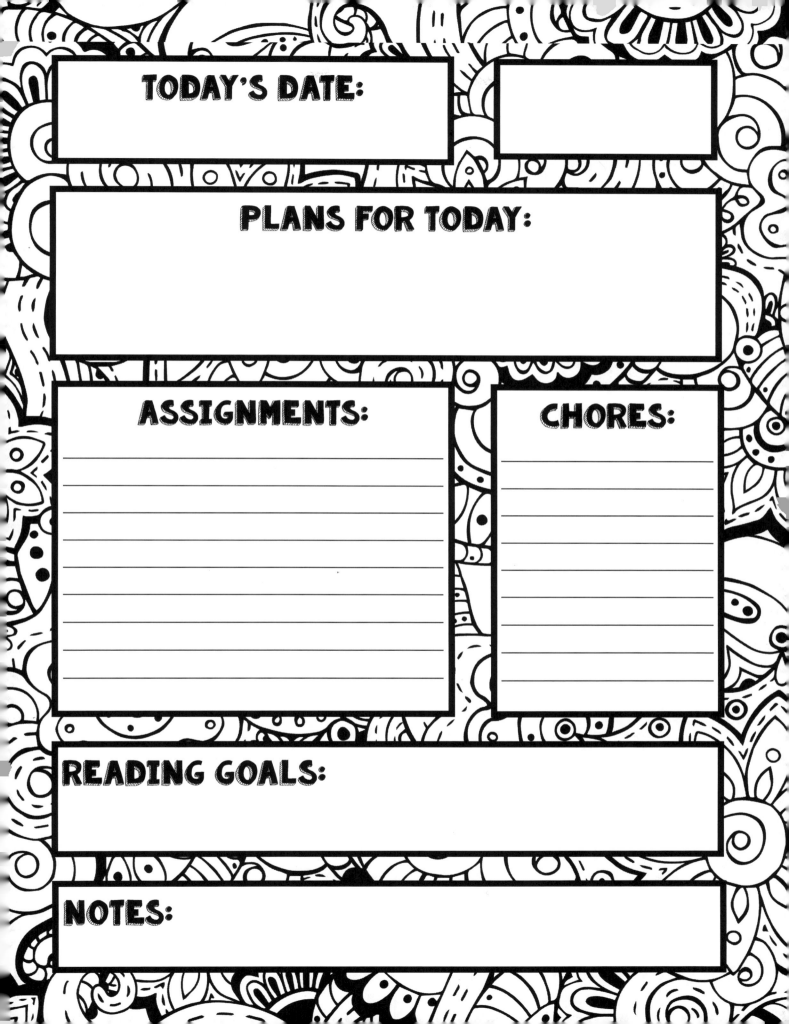

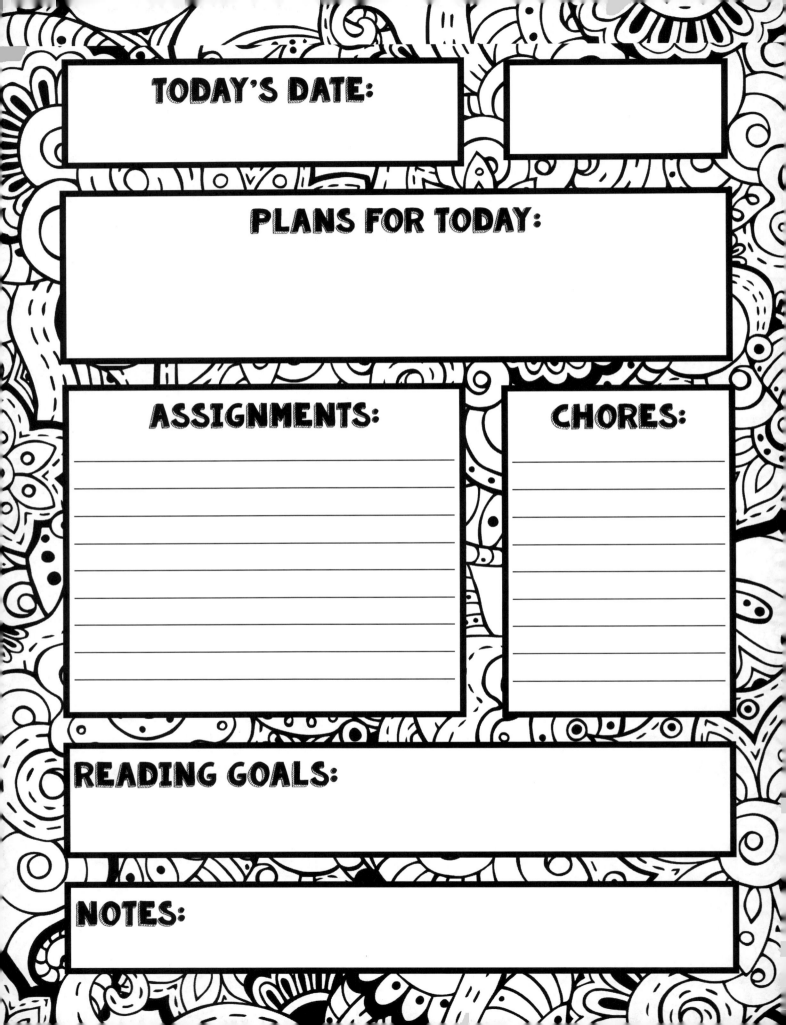

Plans & Perspective

"The home is the first and most effective place to learn the lessons of life: truth, honor, virtue, self control, the value of education, honest work, and the purpose and privilege of life." -McKay

My True Priorities

Long Term Goals

I Am Thankful For...

Checklist

Remember...

_____
_____
_____
_____
_____

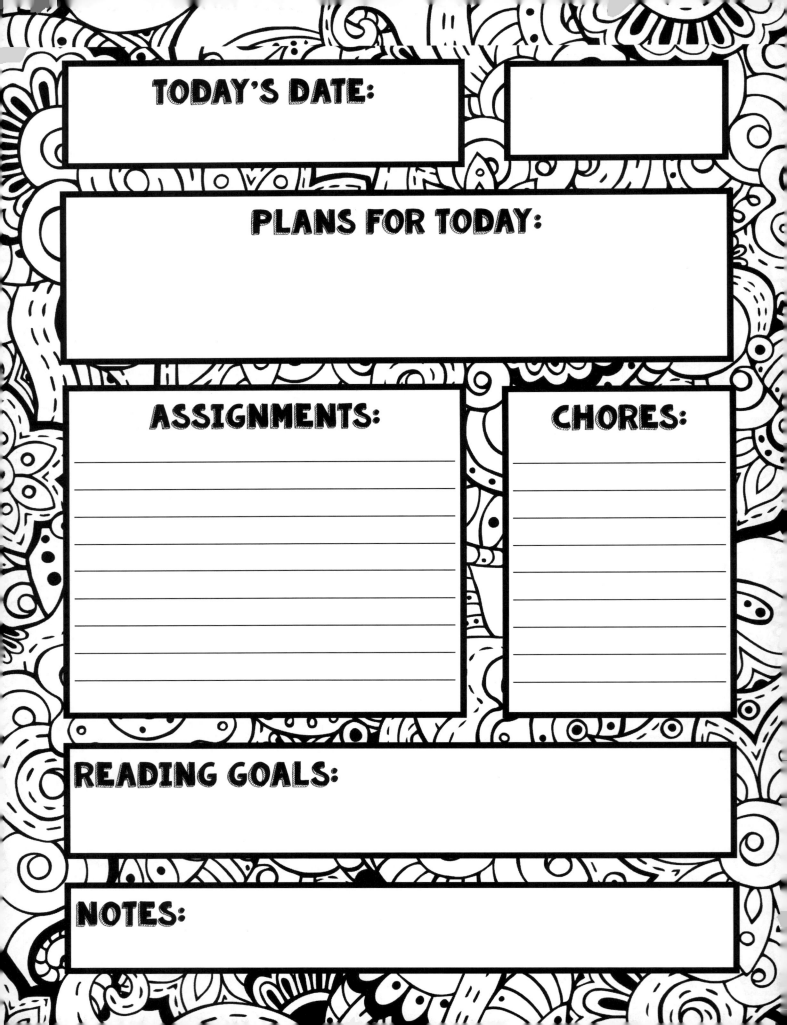

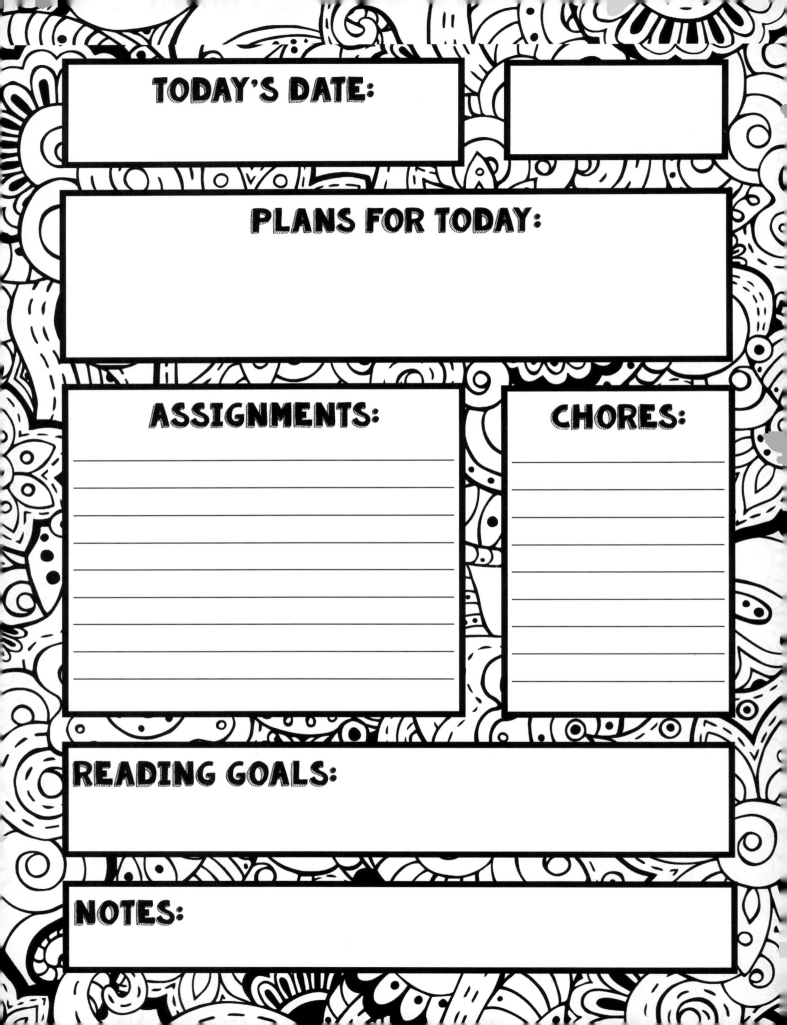

Plans & Perspective

"The home is the first and most effective place to learn the lessons of life: truth, honor, virtue, self control, the value of education, honest work, and the purpose and privilege of life." -McKay

My True Priorities

Long Term Goals

I Am Thankful For...

Checklist

Remember...

_____
_____
_____
_____
_____

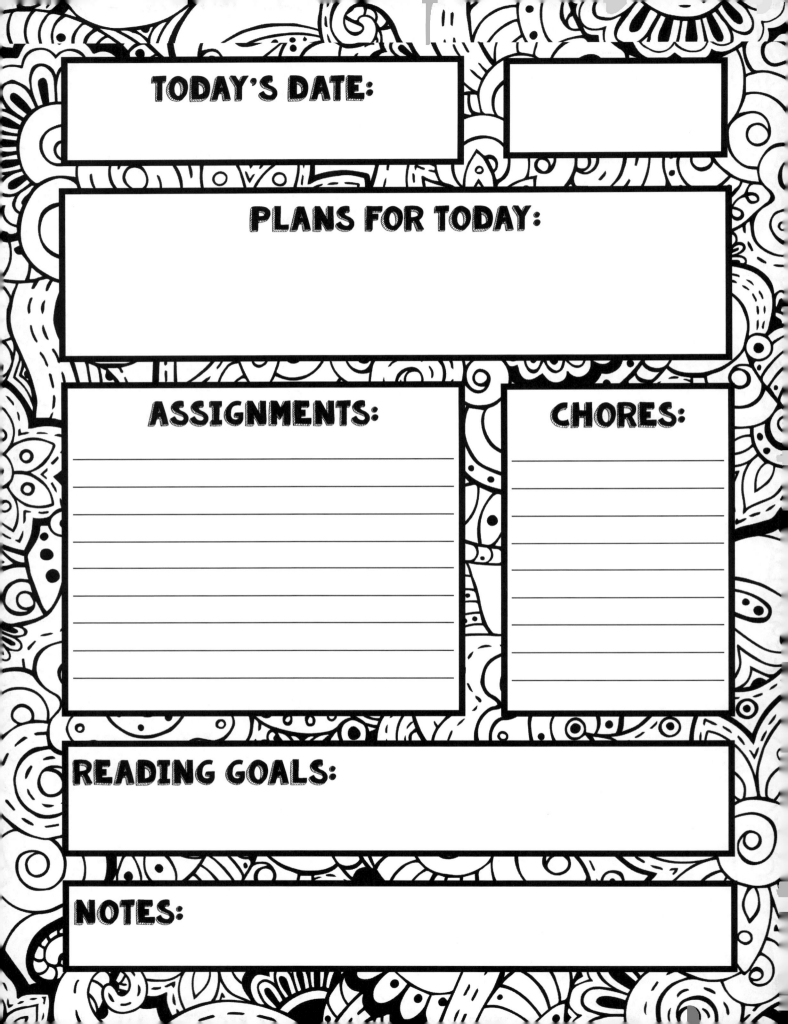

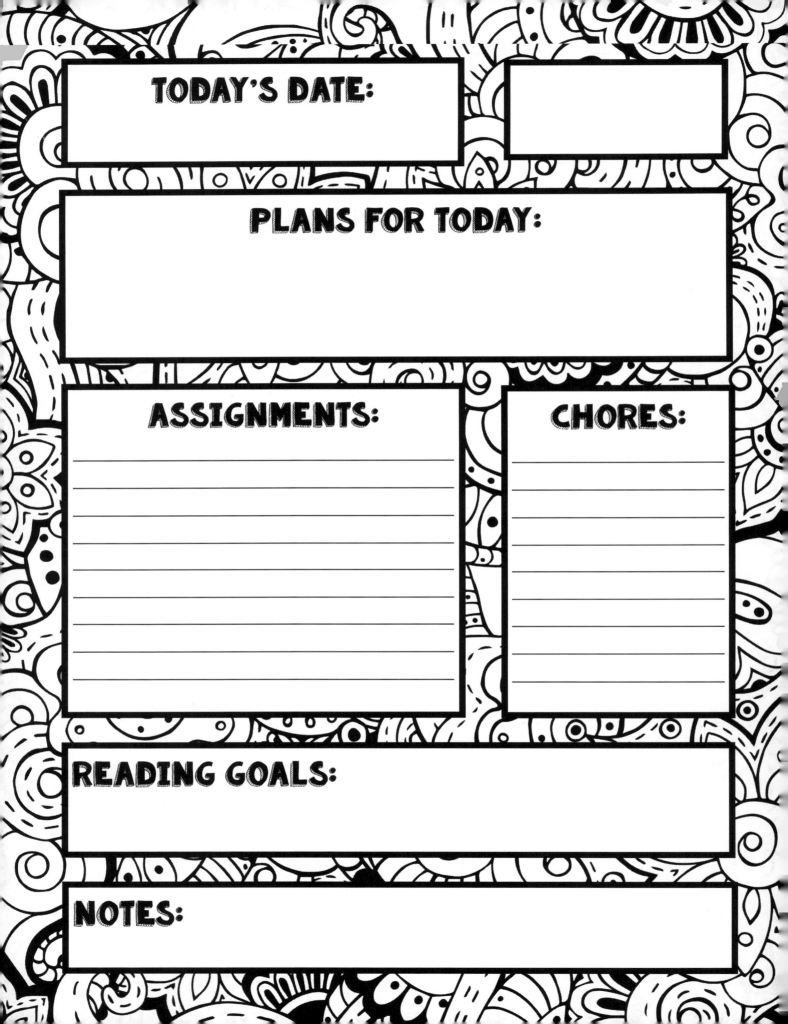

Plans & Perspective

"The home is the first and most effective place to learn the lessons of life: truth, honor, virtue, self control, the value of education, honest work, and the purpose and privilege of life." -McKay

My True Priorities

Long Term Goals

I Am Thankful For...

Checklist

Remember...

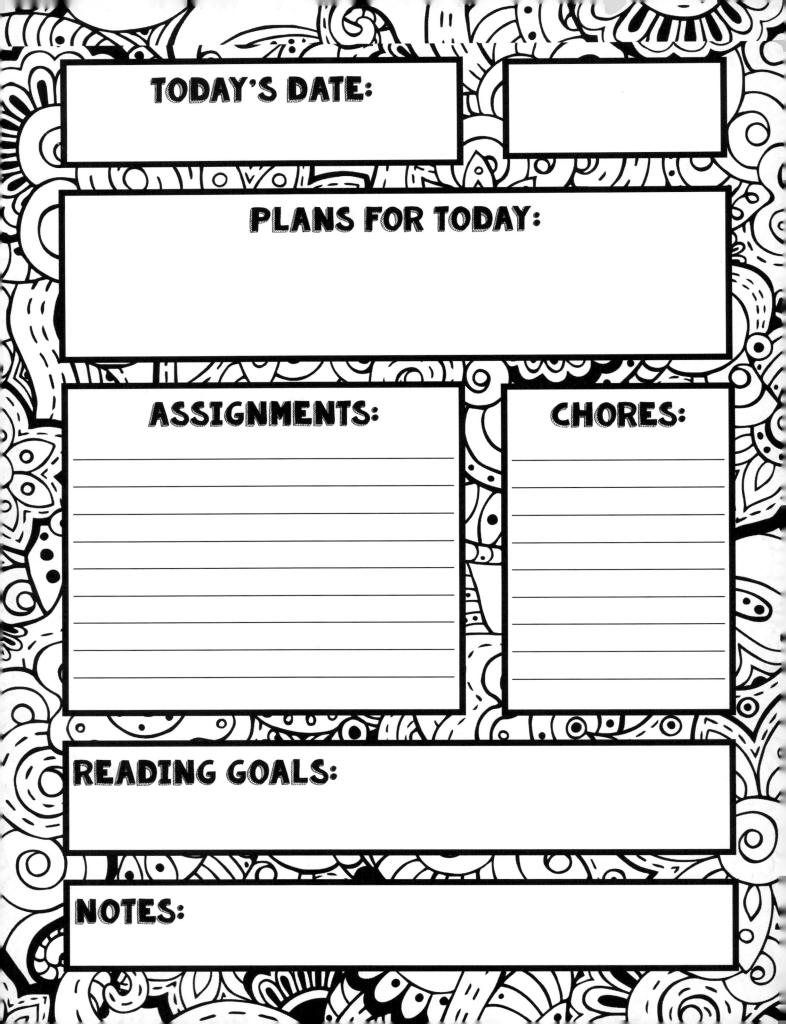

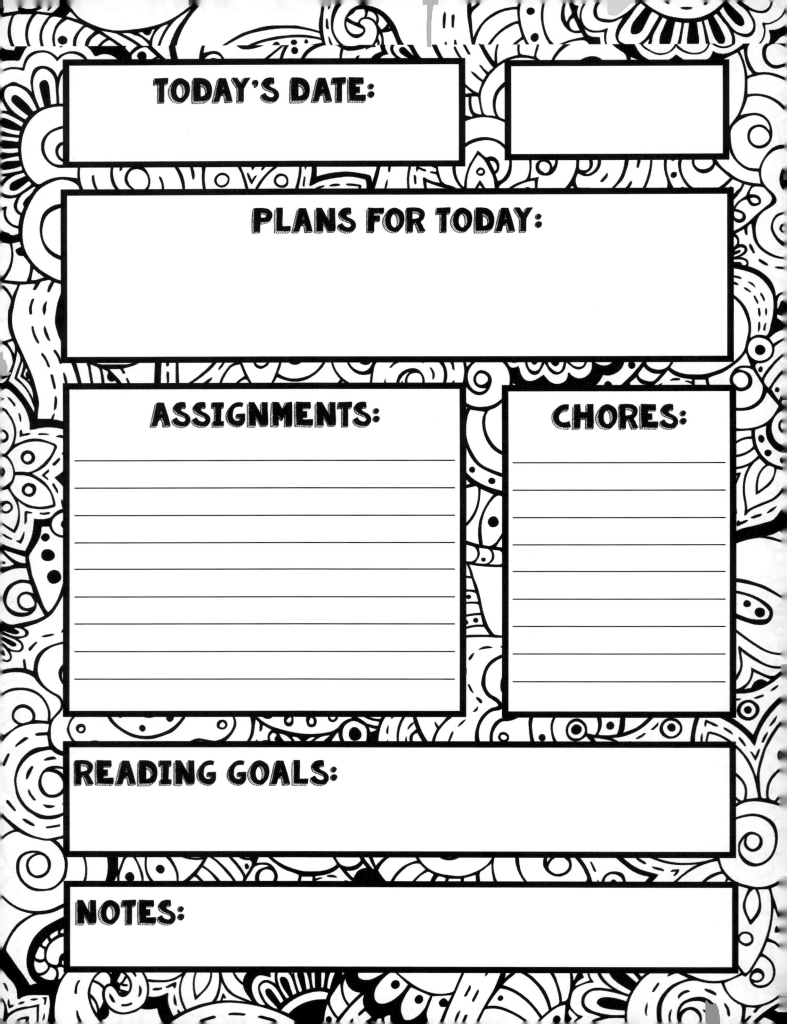

Plans & Perspective

"The home is the first and most effective place to learn the lessons of life: truth, honor, virtue, self control, the value of education, honest work, and the purpose and privilege of life." -McKay

My True Priorities

Long Term Goals

I Am Thankful For...

Checklist

Remember...

_____
_____
_____
_____
_____

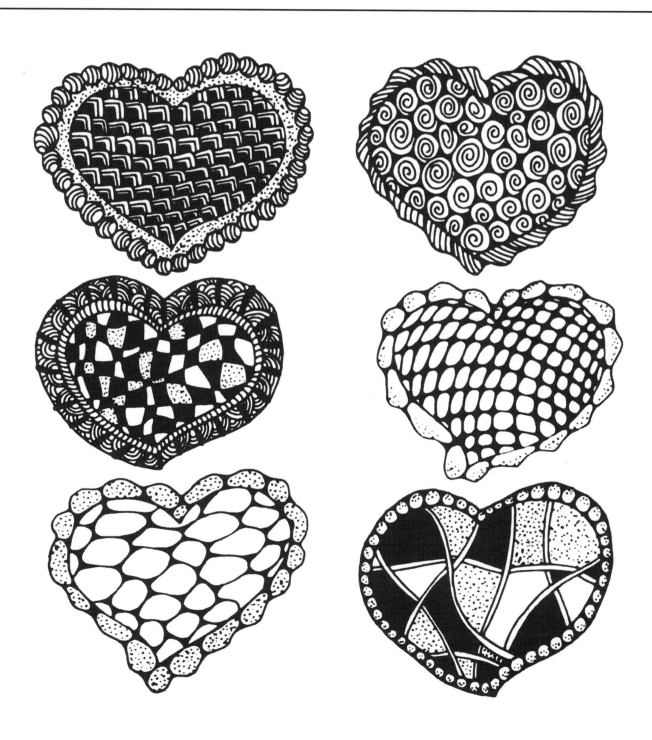

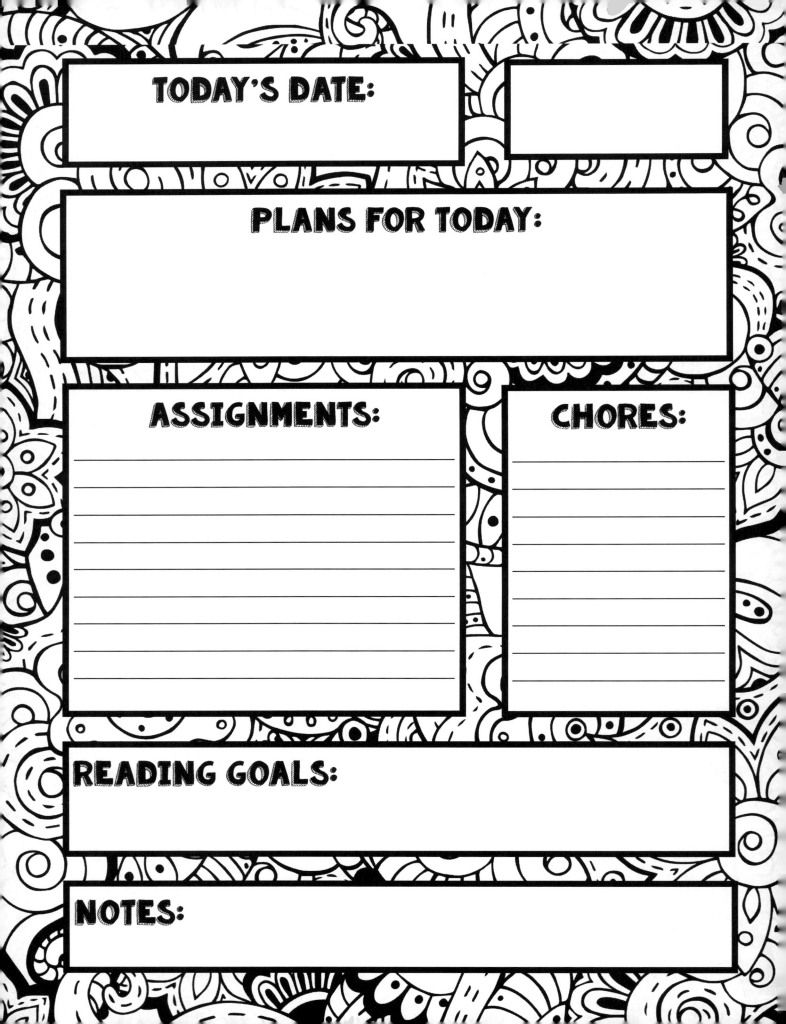

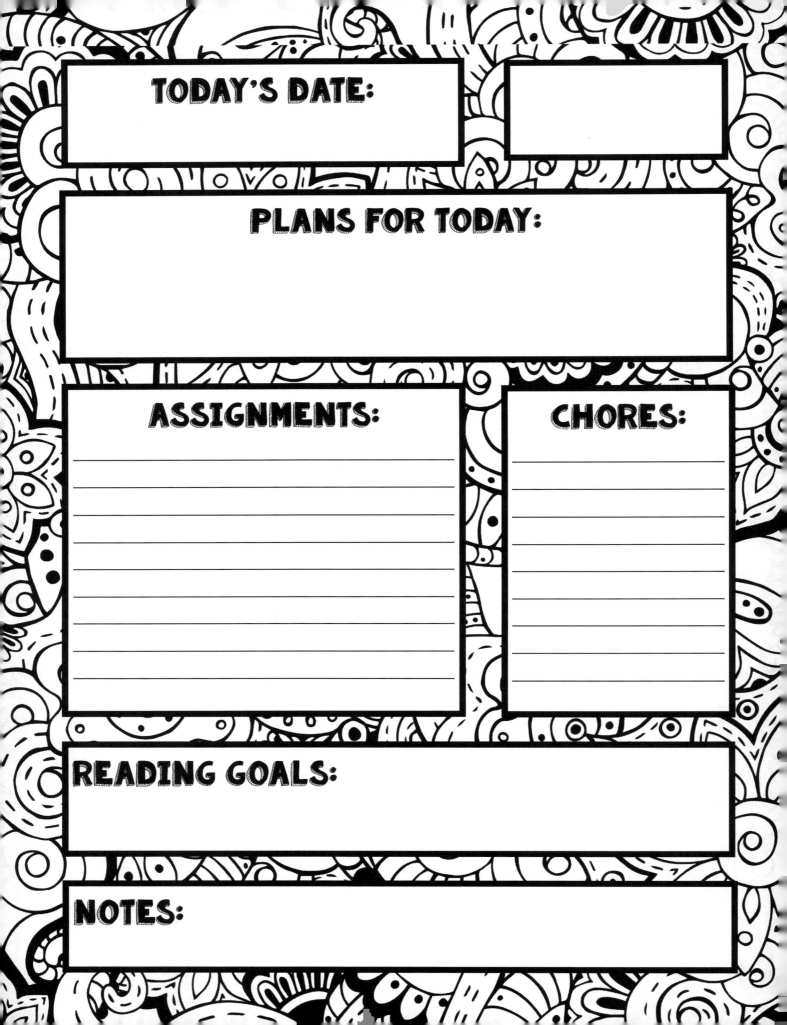

Plans & Perspective

"The home is the first and most effective place to learn the lessons of life: truth, honor, virtue, self control, the value of education, honest work, and the purpose and privilege of life." -McKay

My True Priorities

Long Term Goals

I Am Thankful For...

Checklist

Remember...

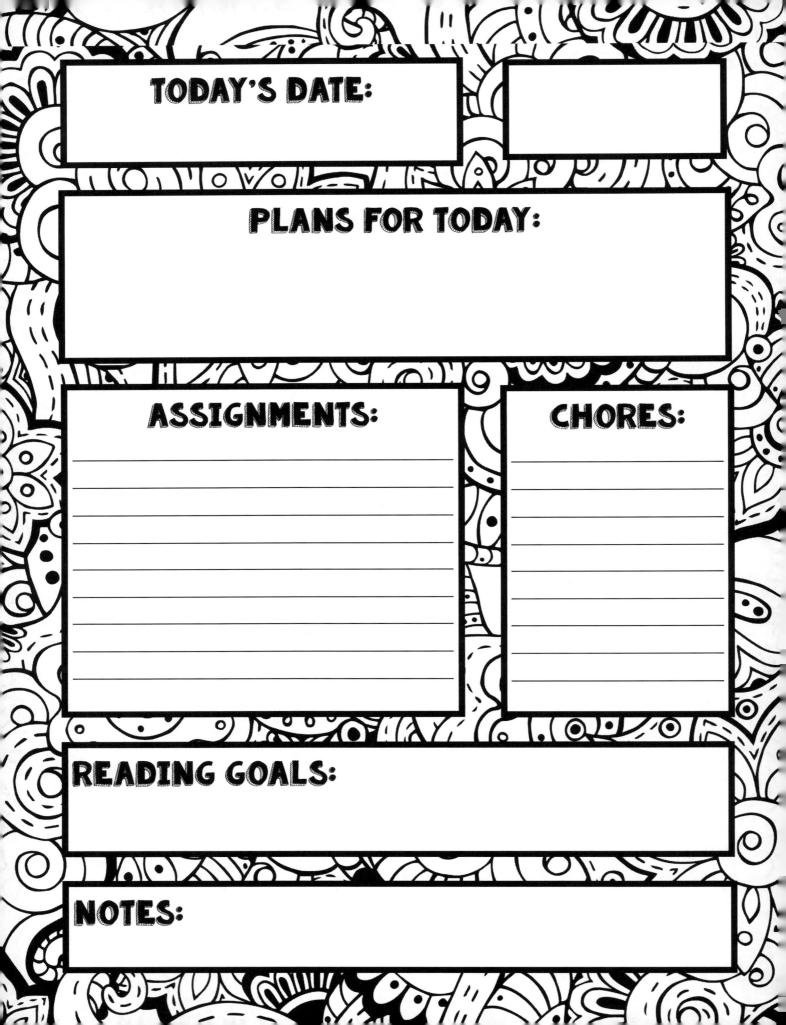

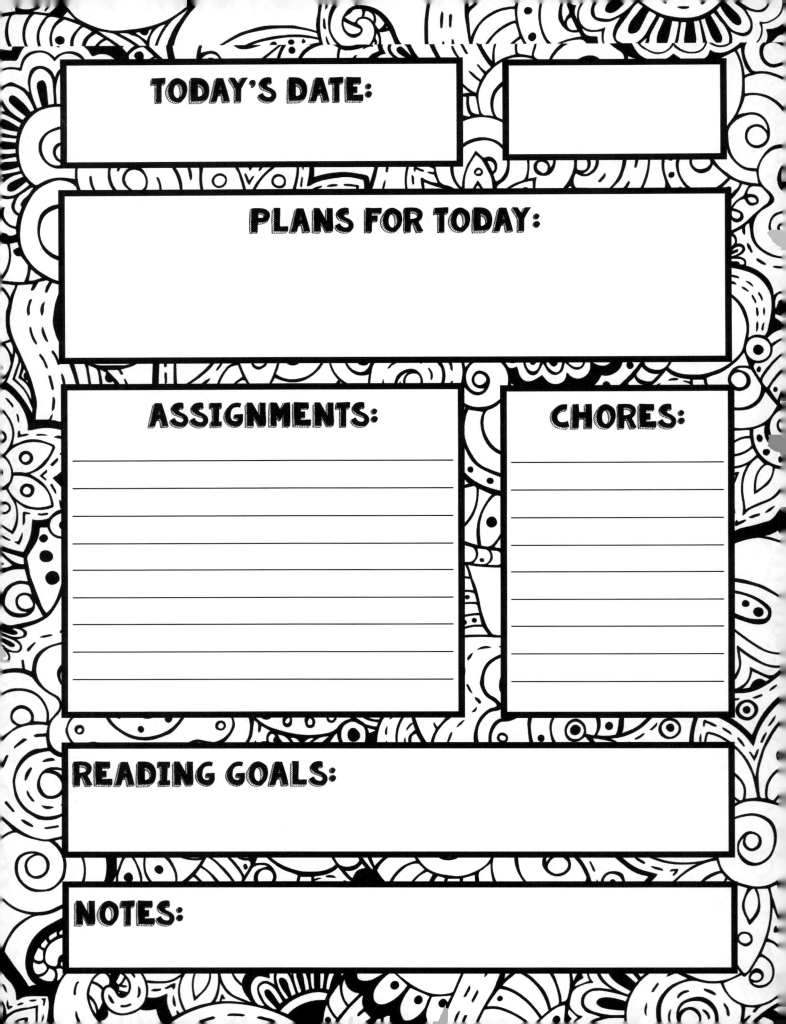

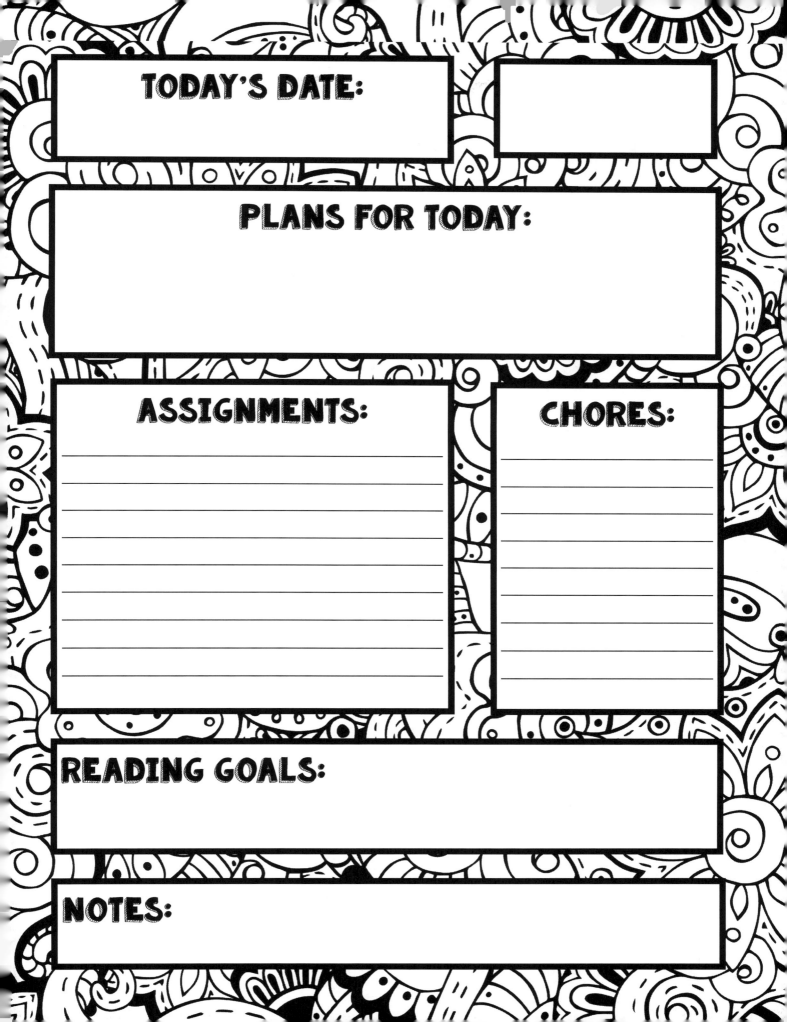

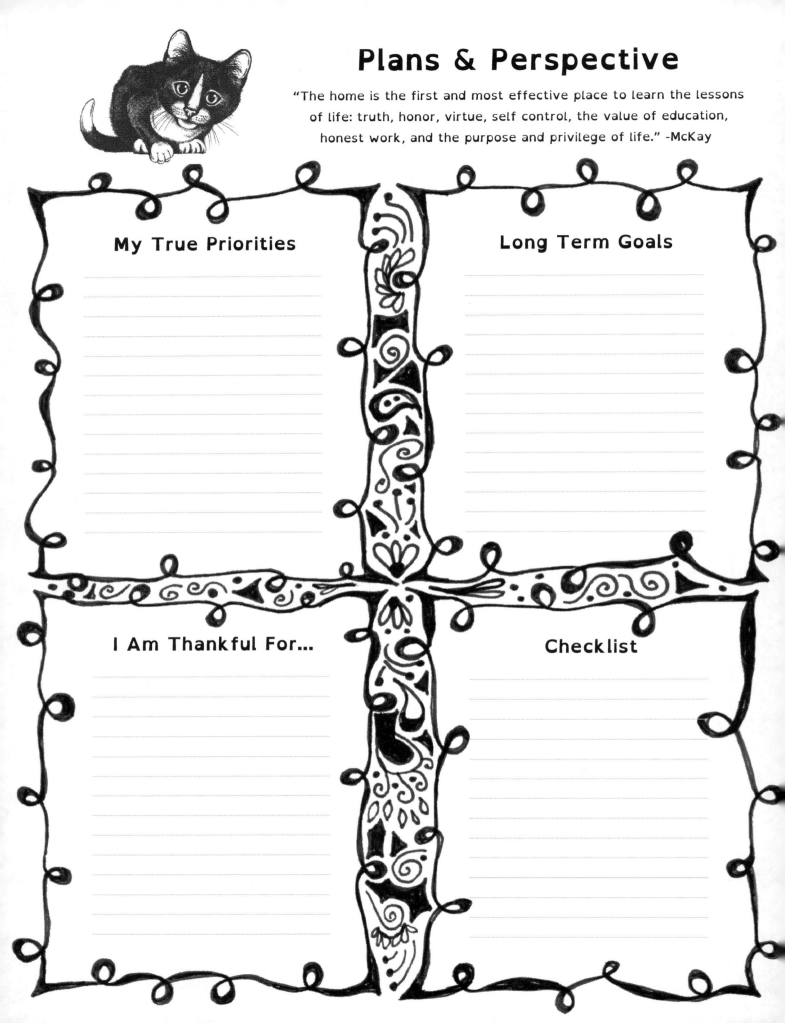

Plans & Perspective

"The home is the first and most effective place to learn the lessons of life: truth, honor, virtue, self control, the value of education, honest work, and the purpose and privilege of life." -McKay

My True Priorities

Long Term Goals

I Am Thankful For...

Checklist

Remember...

_____
_____
_____
_____
_____

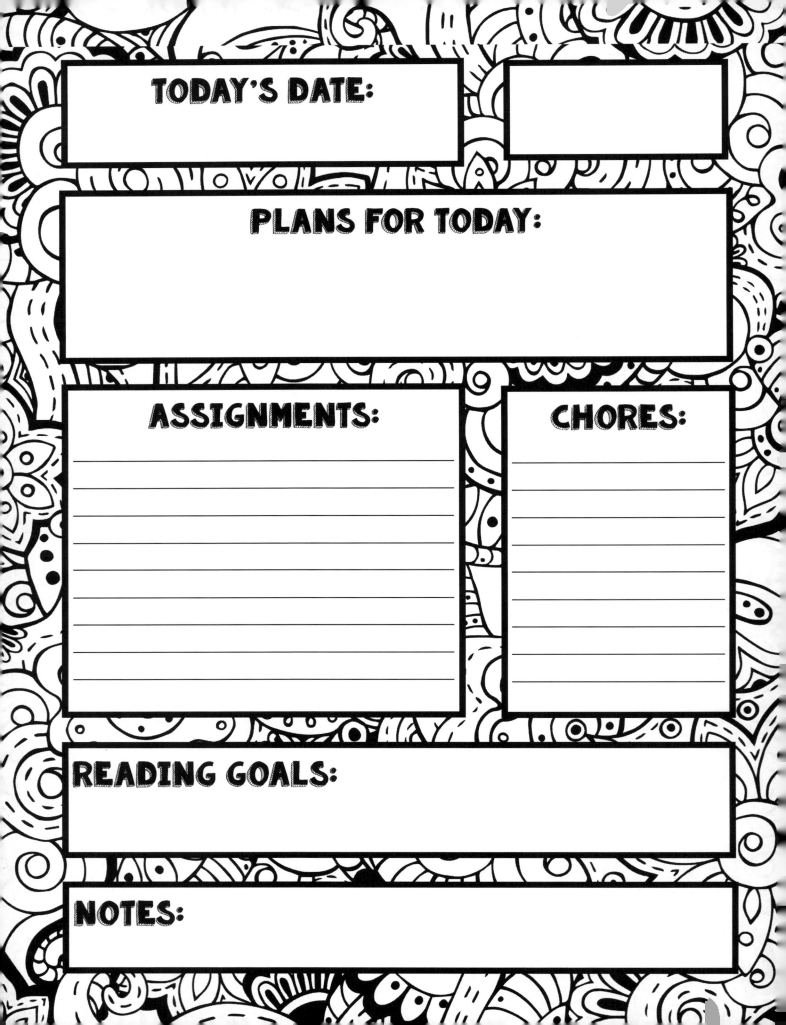

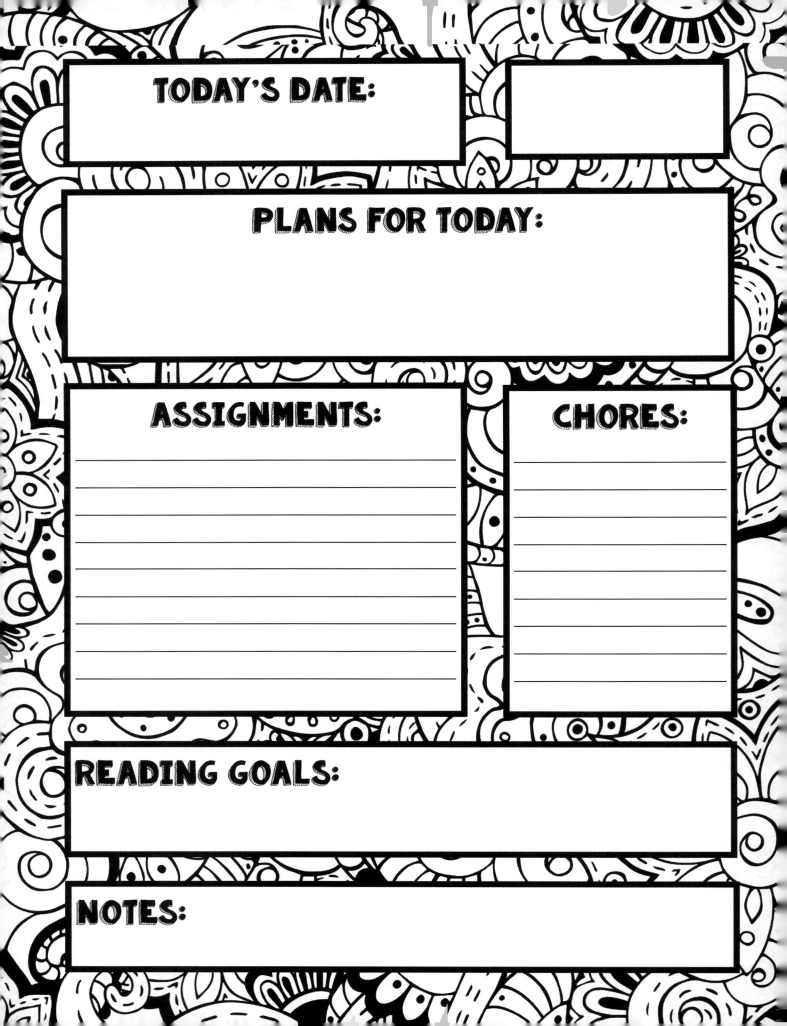

Plans & Perspective

"The home is the first and most effective place to learn the lessons of life: truth, honor, virtue, self control, the value of education, honest work, and the purpose and privilege of life." -McKay

My True Priorities

Long Term Goals

I Am Thankful For...

Checklist

Remember...

_____
_____
_____
_____
_____

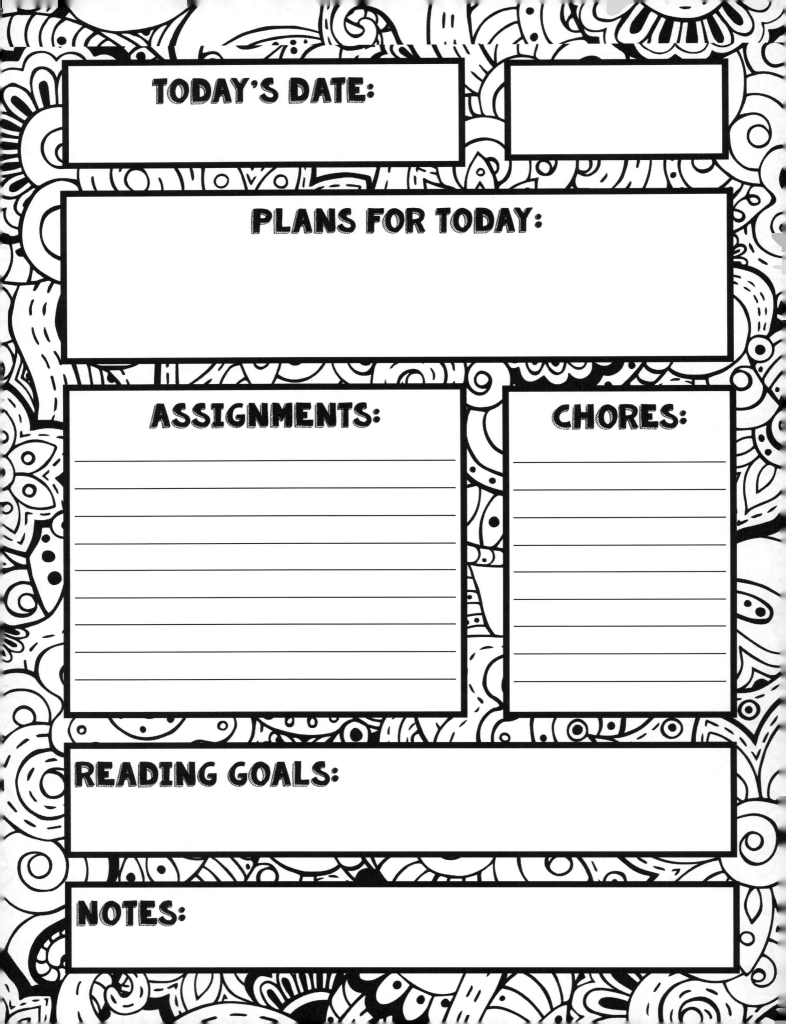

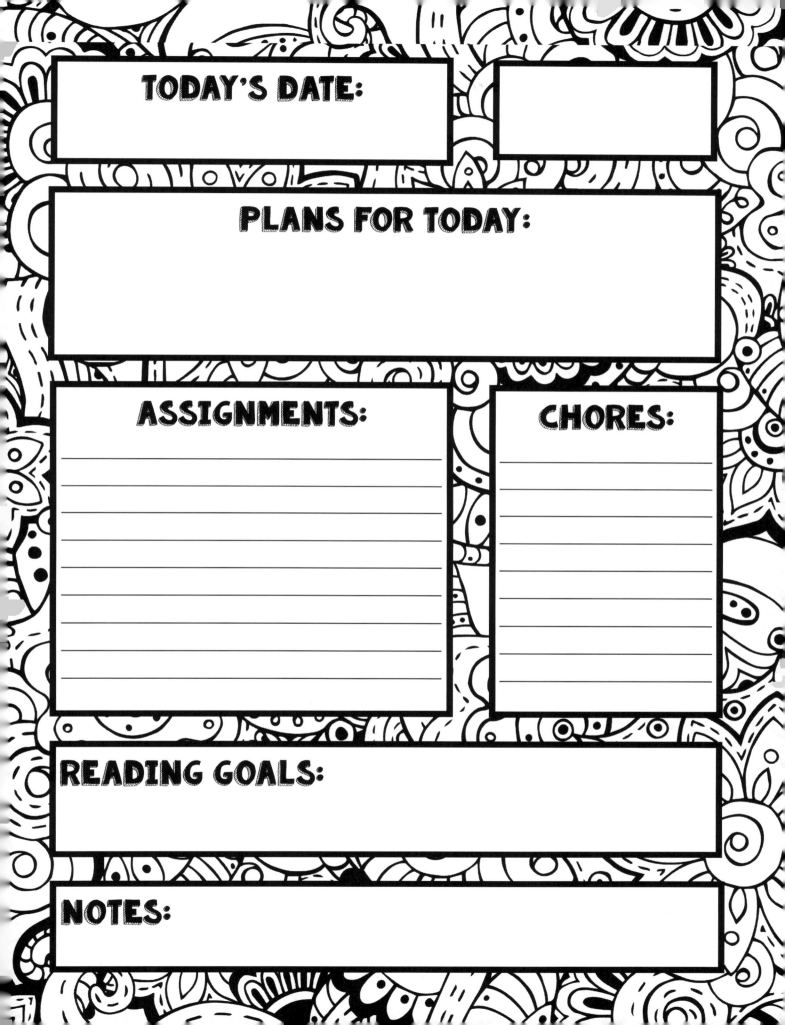

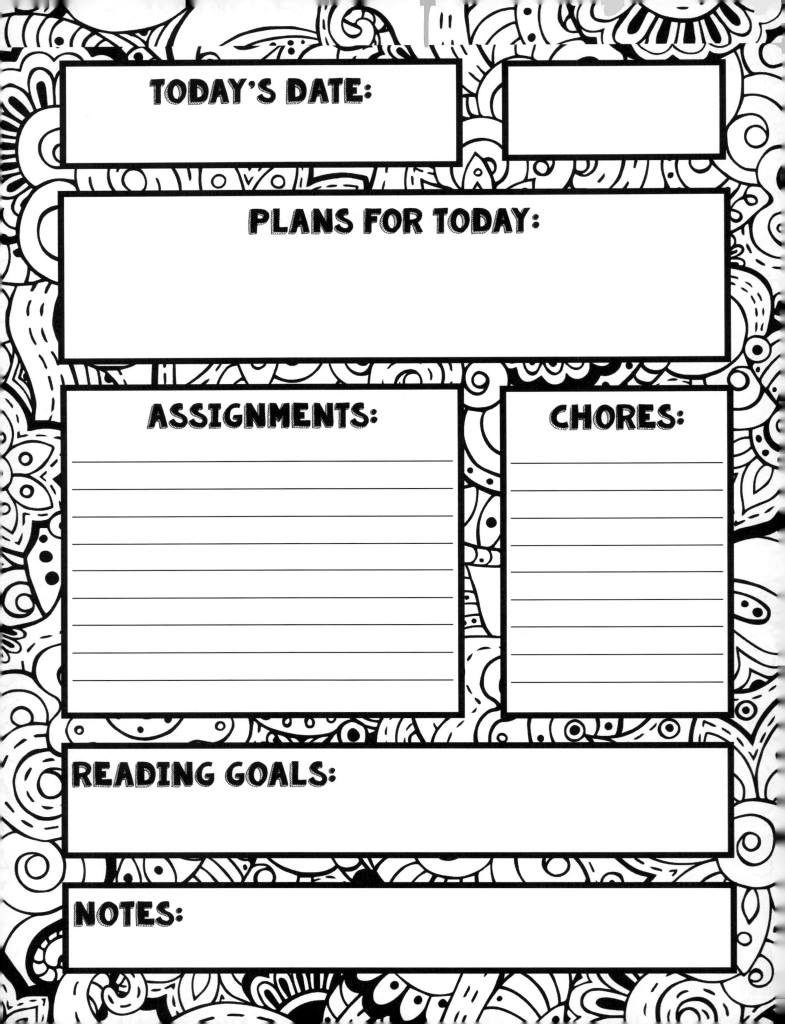

Plans & Perspective

"The home is the first and most effective place to learn the lessons of life: truth, honor, virtue, self control, the value of education, honest work, and the purpose and privilege of life." -McKay

My True Priorities

Long Term Goals

I Am Thankful For...

Checklist

Remember...

_____
_____
_____
_____
_____

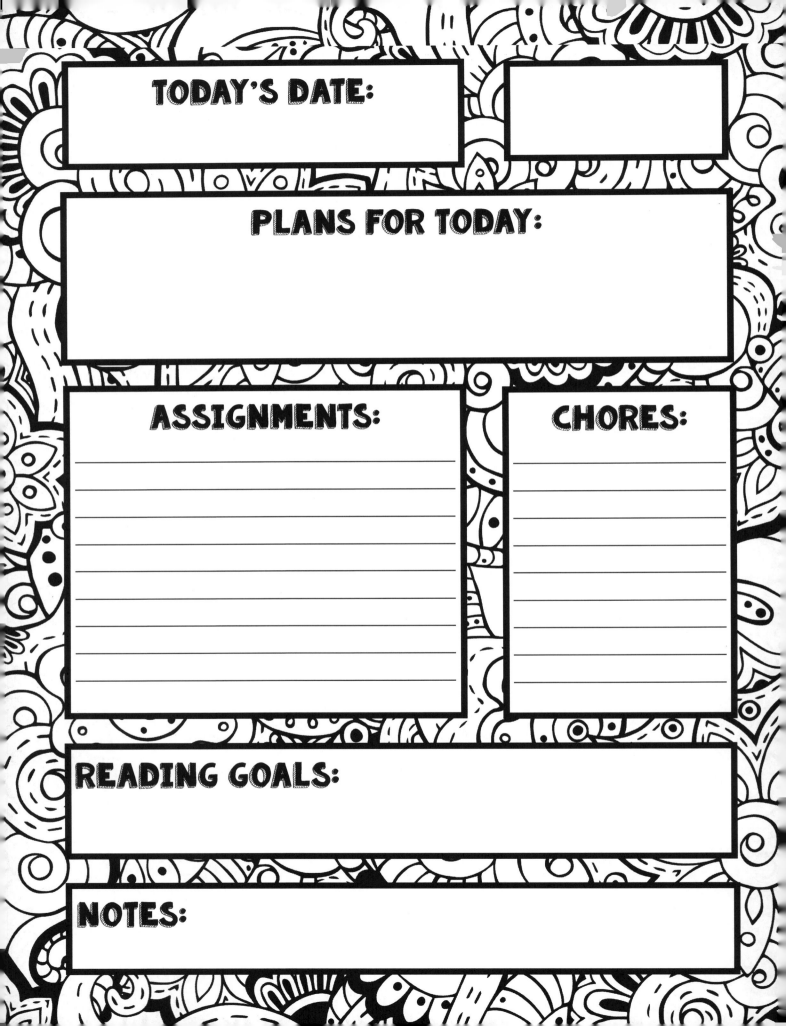

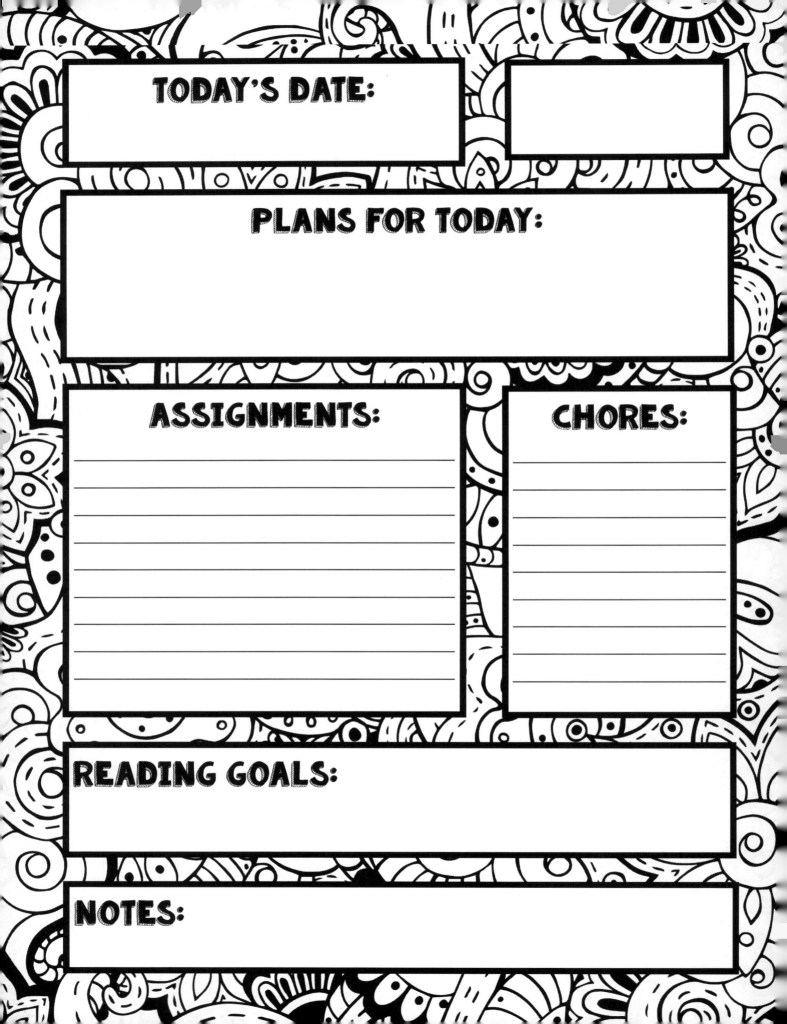

Plans & Perspective

"The home is the first and most effective place to learn the lessons of life: truth, honor, virtue, self control, the value of education, honest work, and the purpose and privilege of life." -McKay

My True Priorities

Long Term Goals

I Am Thankful For...

Checklist

Remember...

_____
_____
_____
_____
_____

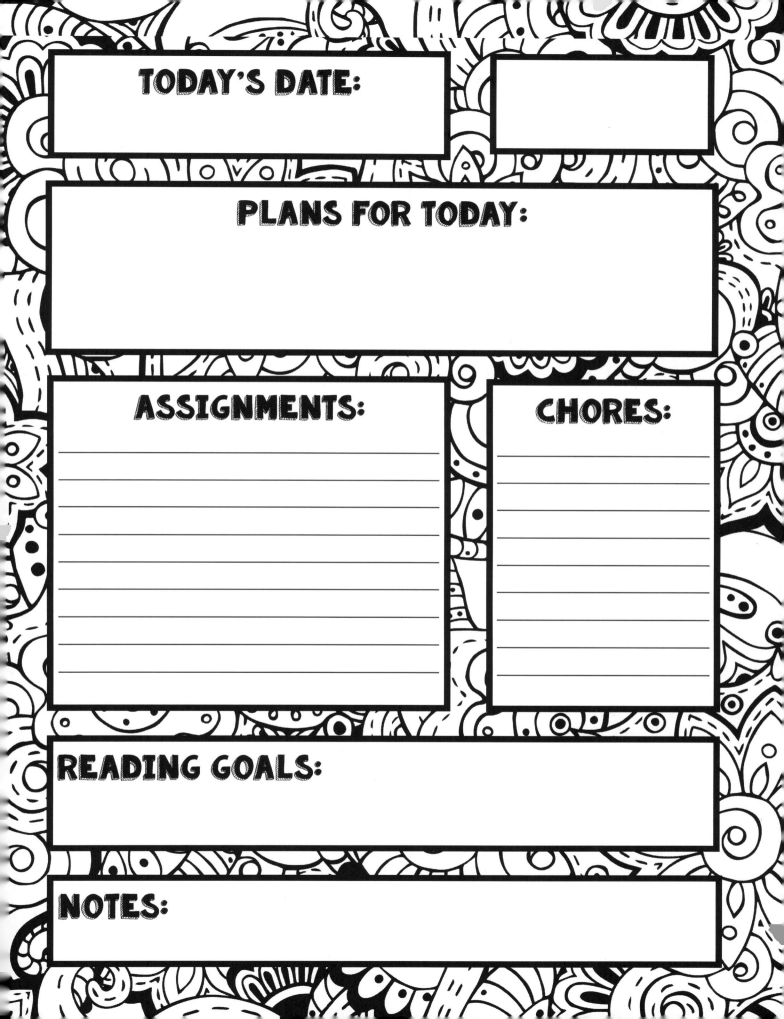

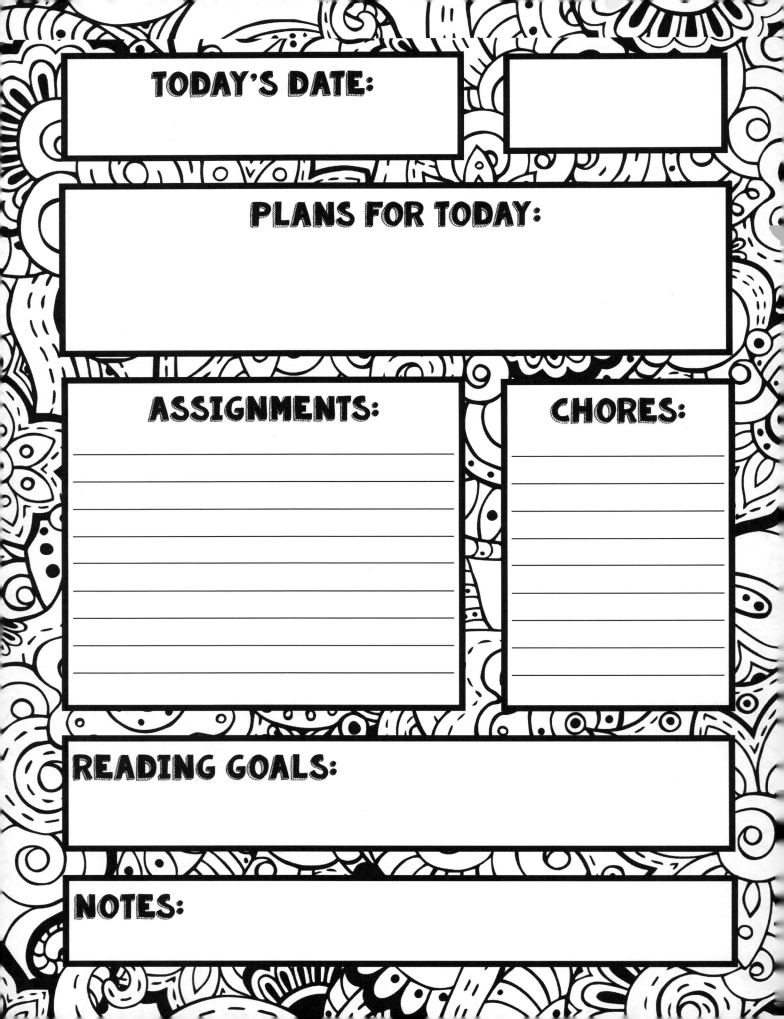

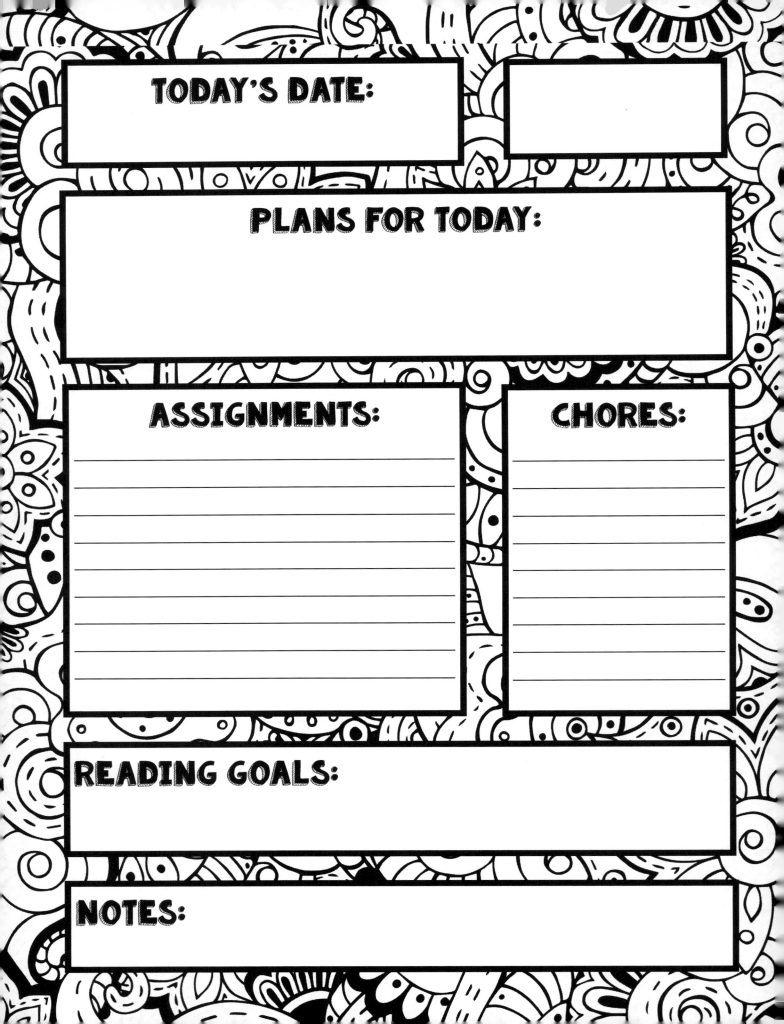

Plans & Perspective

"The home is the first and most effective place to learn the lessons of life: truth, honor, virtue, self control, the value of education, honest work, and the purpose and privilege of life." -McKay

My True Priorities

Long Term Goals

I Am Thankful For...

Checklist

Remember...

_____
_____
_____
_____
_____

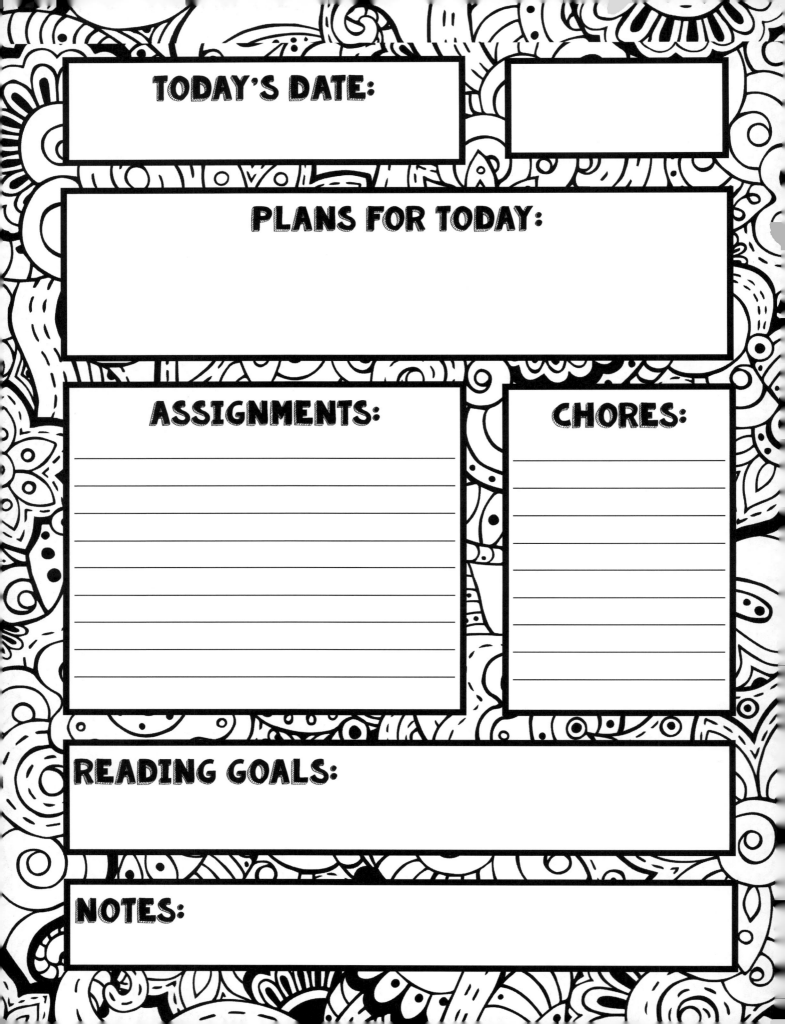

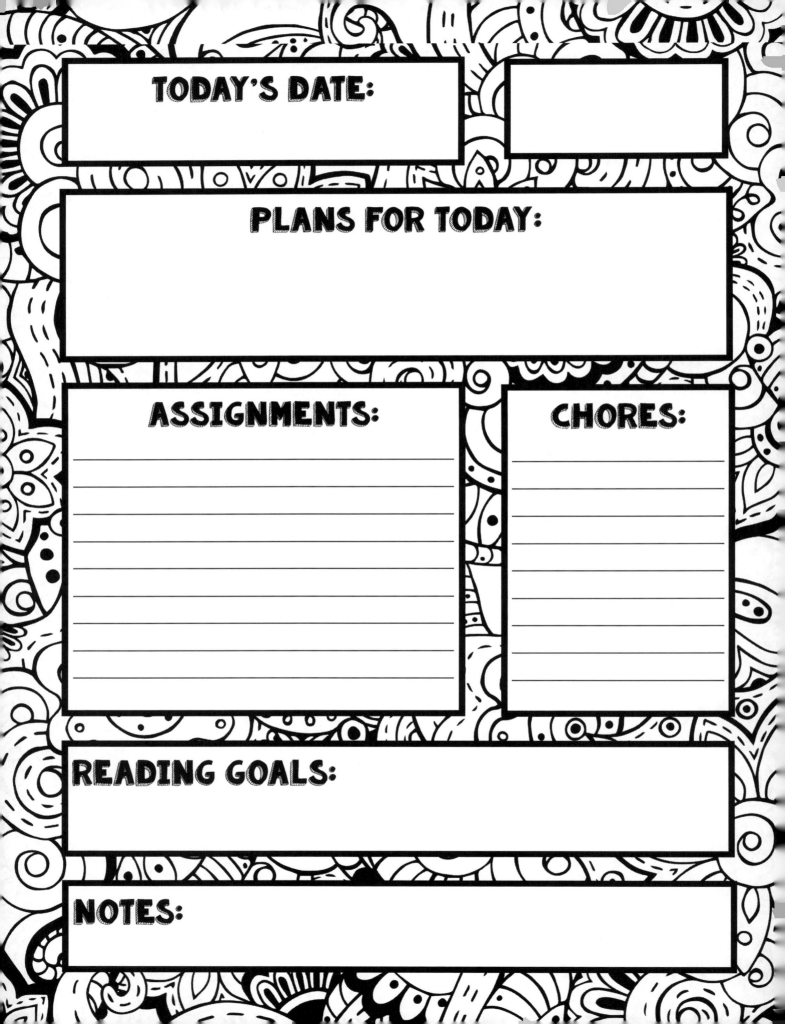

Plans & Perspective

"The home is the first and most effective place to learn the lessons of life: truth, honor, virtue, self control, the value of education, honest work, and the purpose and privilege of life." -McKay

My True Priorities

Long Term Goals

I Am Thankful For...

Checklist

Remember...

_____
_____
_____
_____
_____

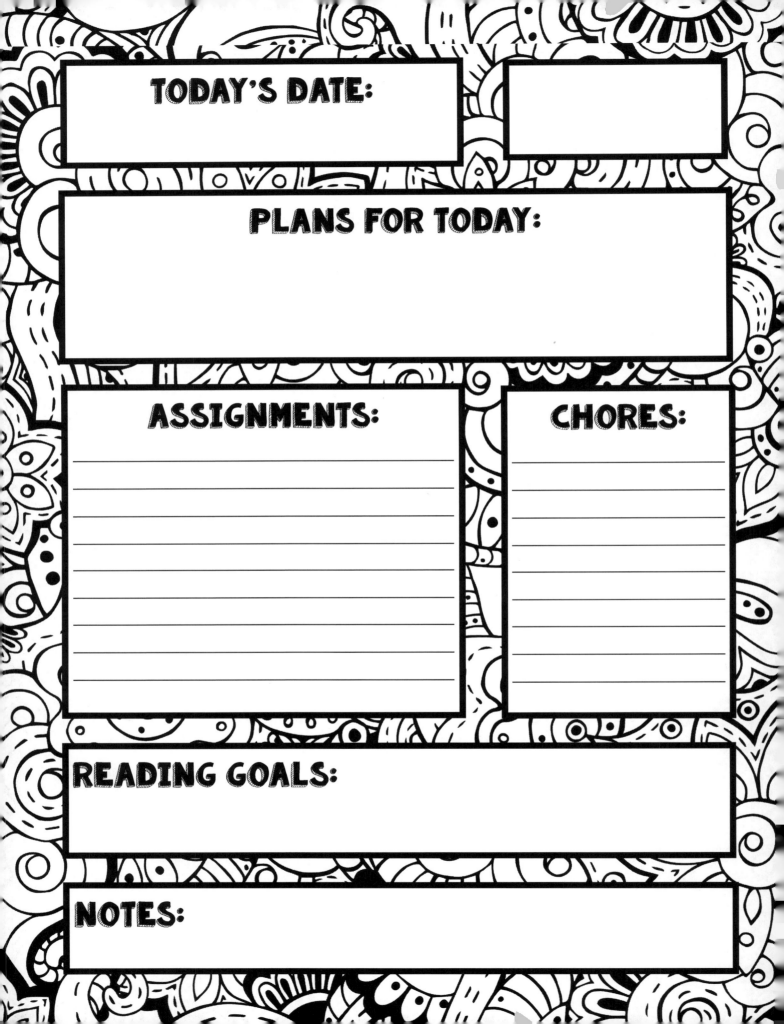

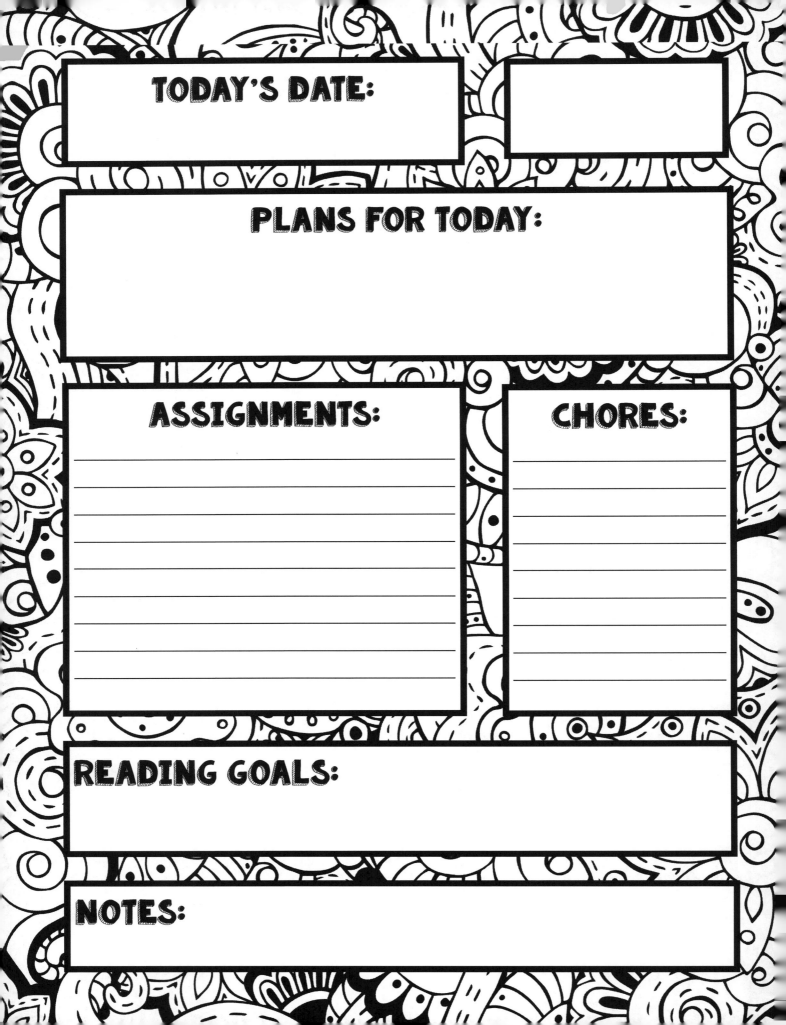

Plans & Perspective

"The home is the first and most effective place to learn the lessons of life: truth, honor, virtue, self control, the value of education, honest work, and the purpose and privilege of life." -McKay

My True Priorities

Long Term Goals

I Am Thankful For...

Checklist

Remember...

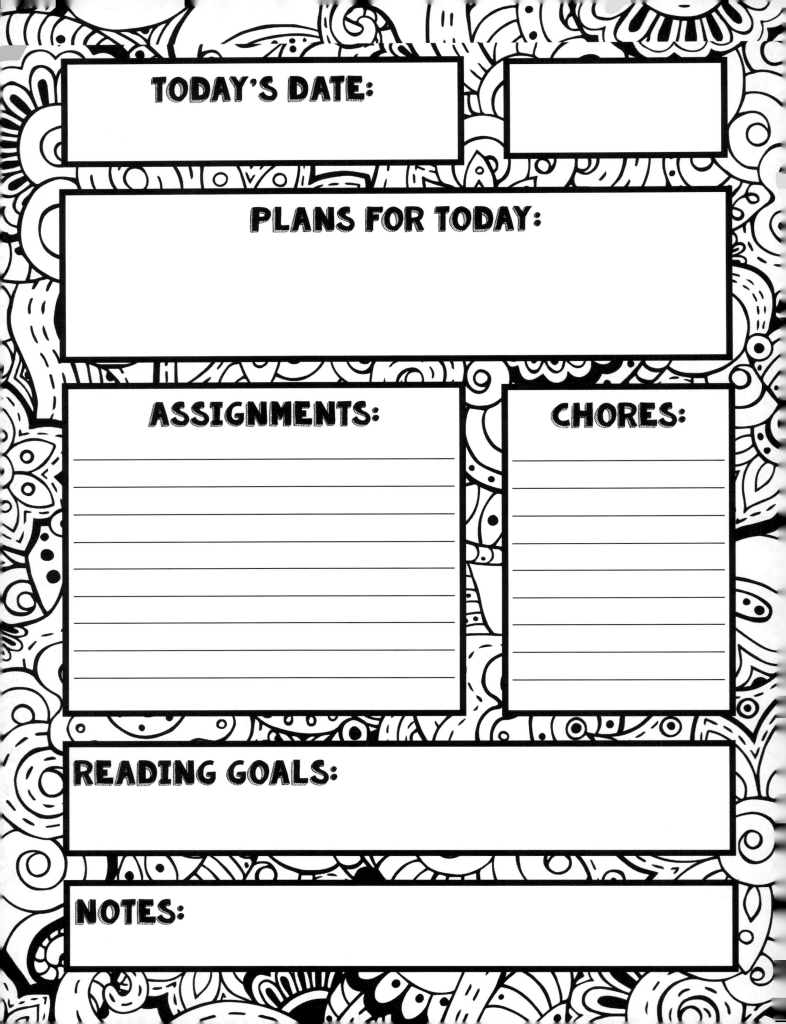

TODAY'S DATE:

PLANS FOR TODAY:

ASSIGNMENTS:

CHORES:

READING GOALS:

NOTES:

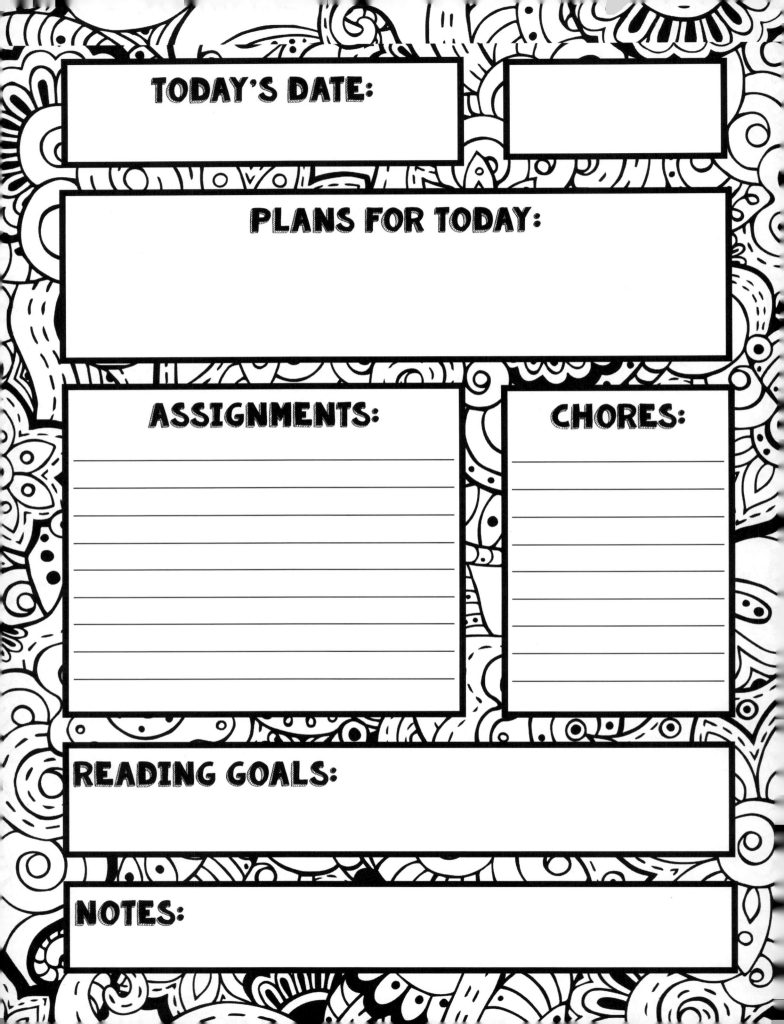

Plans & Perspective

"The home is the first and most effective place to learn the lessons of life: truth, honor, virtue, self control, the value of education, honest work, and the purpose and privilege of life." -McKay

My True Priorities

Long Term Goals

I Am Thankful For...

Checklist

Remember...

_____
_____
_____
_____
_____

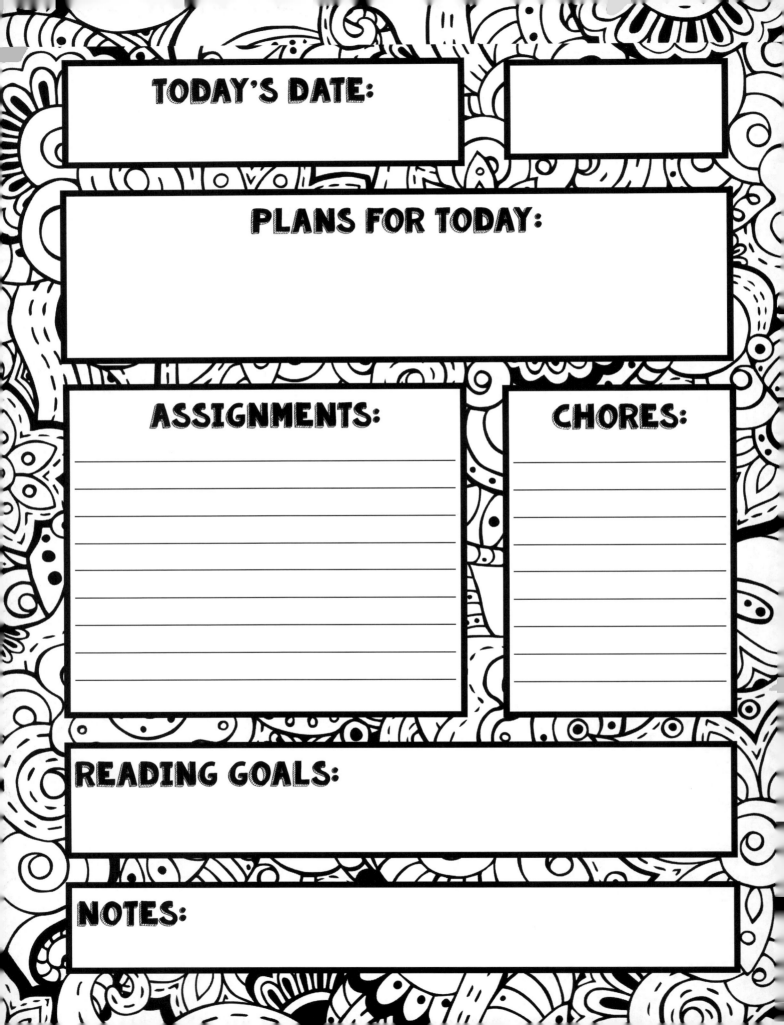

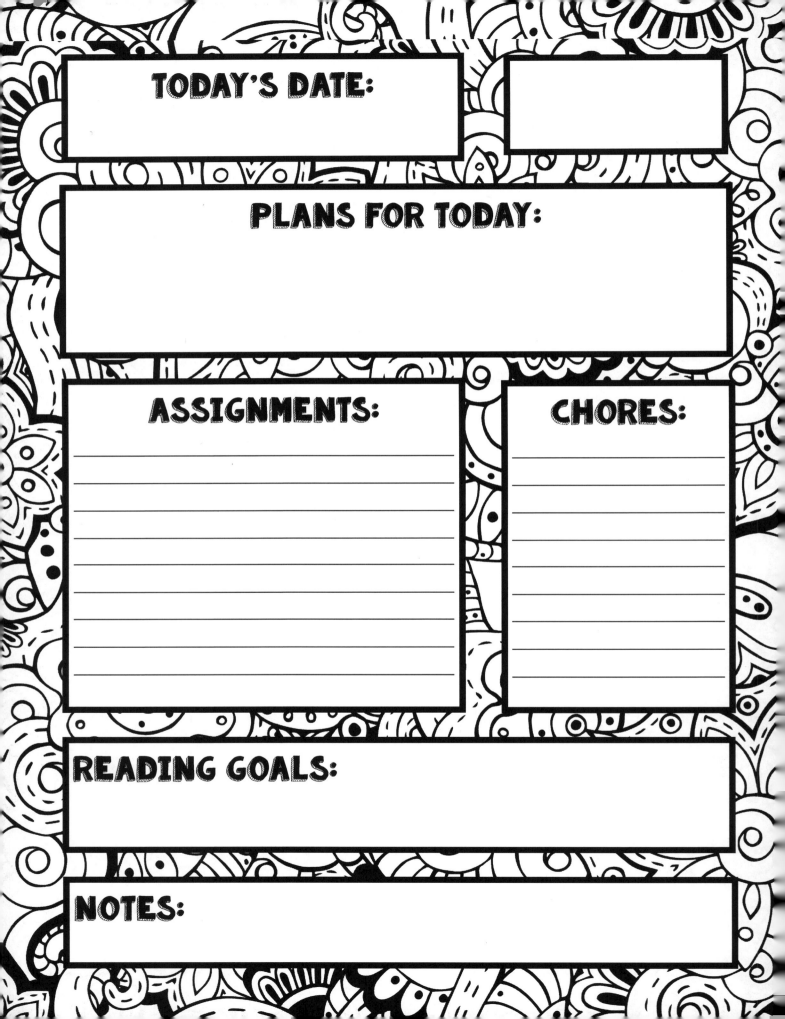

Plans & Perspective

"The home is the first and most effective place to learn the lessons of life: truth, honor, virtue, self control, the value of education, honest work, and the purpose and privilege of life." -McKay

My True Priorities

Long Term Goals

I Am Thankful For...

Checklist

Remember...

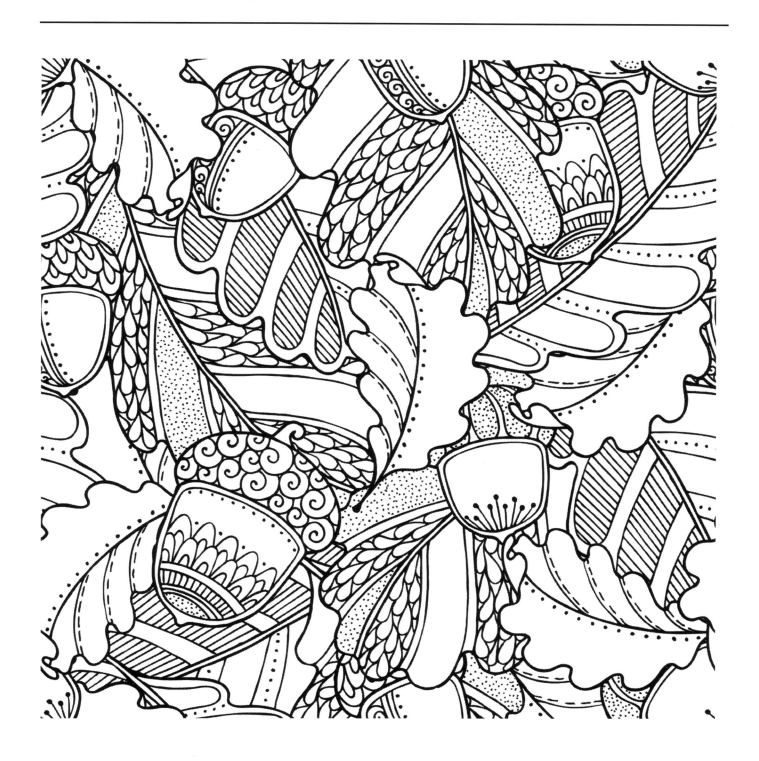

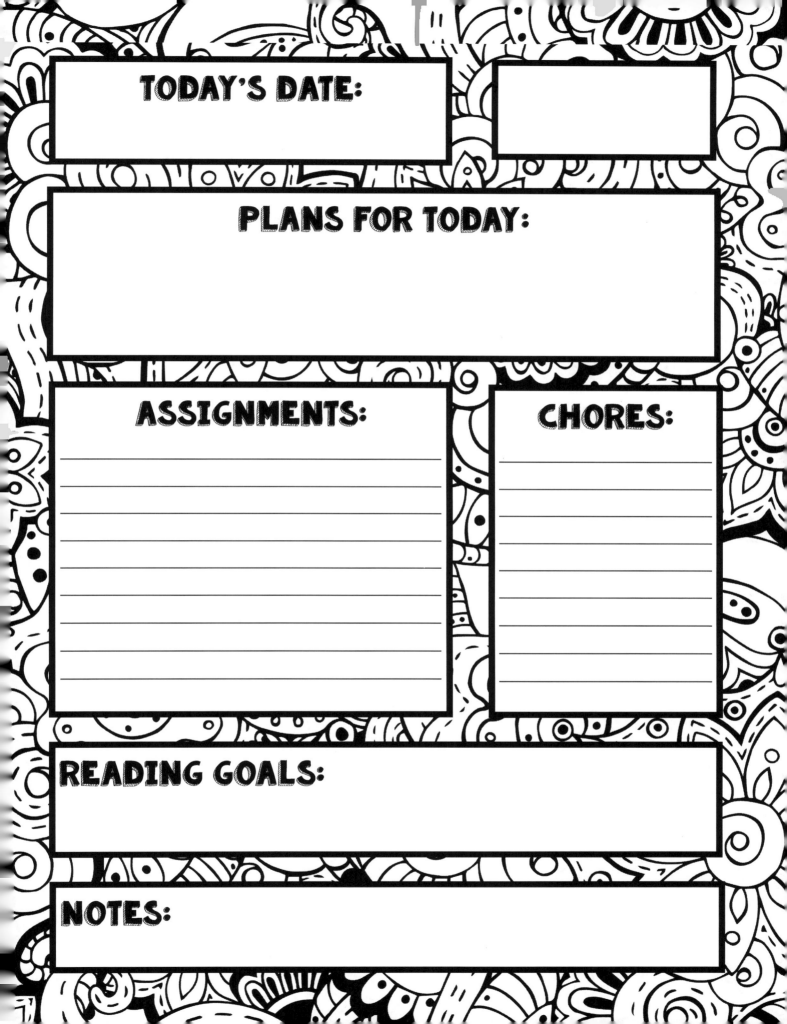

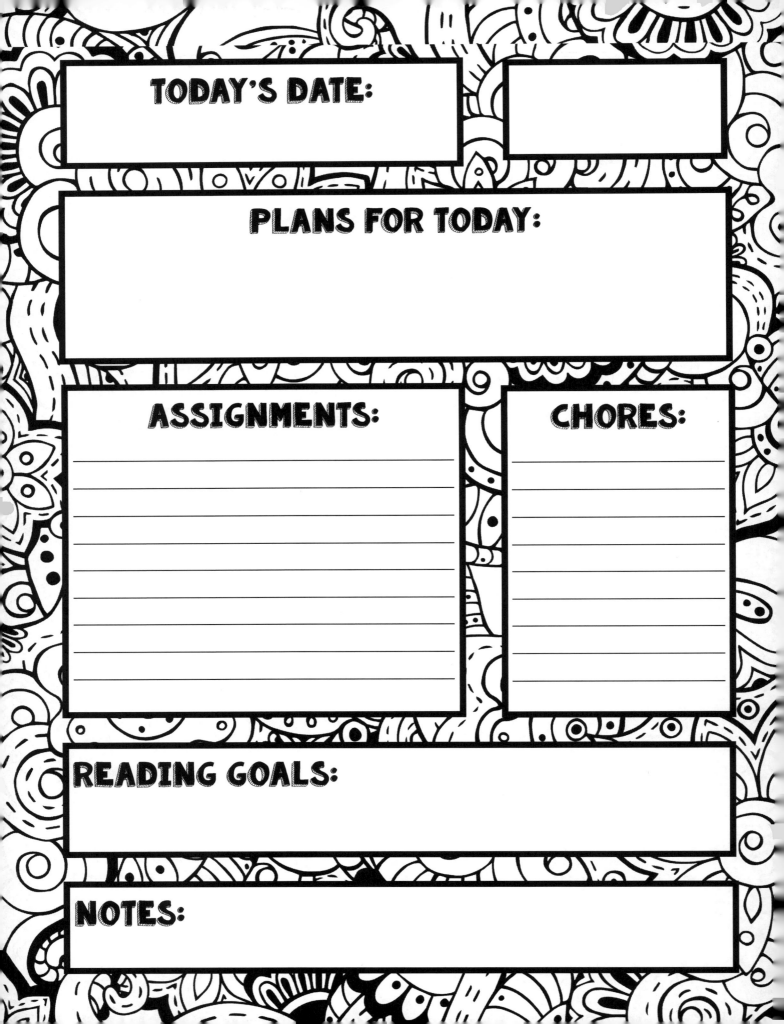

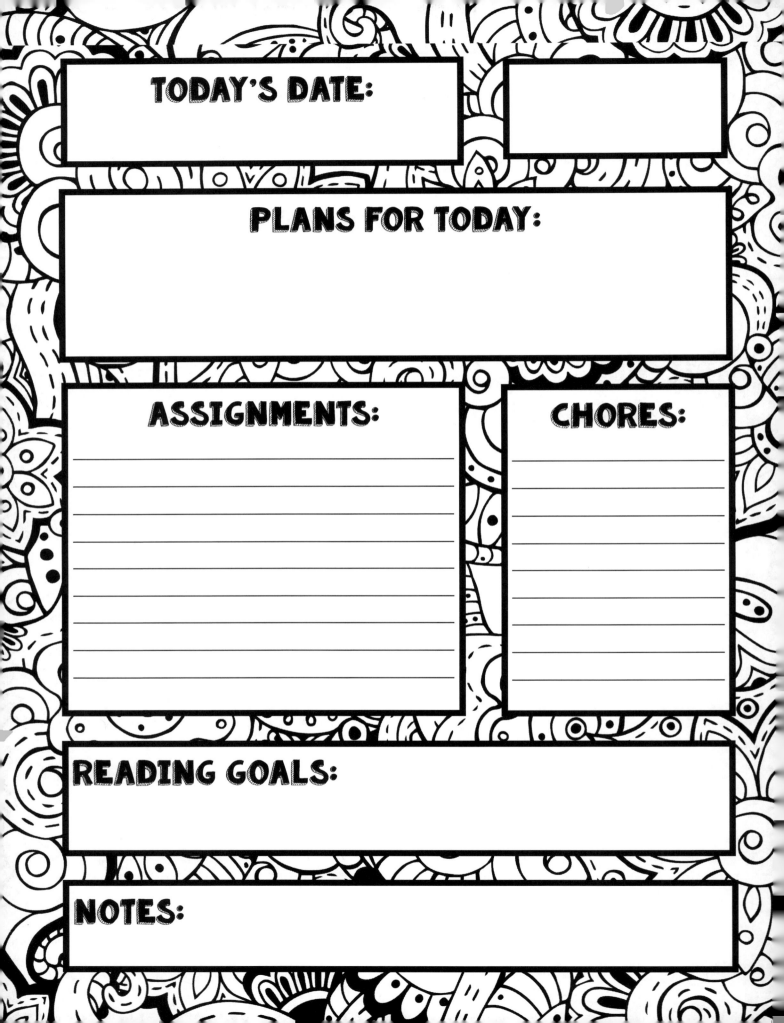

Plans & Perspective

"The home is the first and most effective place to learn the lessons of life: truth, honor, virtue, self control, the value of education, honest work, and the purpose and privilege of life." -McKay

My True Priorities

Long Term Goals

I Am Thankful For...

Checklist

Remember...

_____
_____
_____
_____
_____

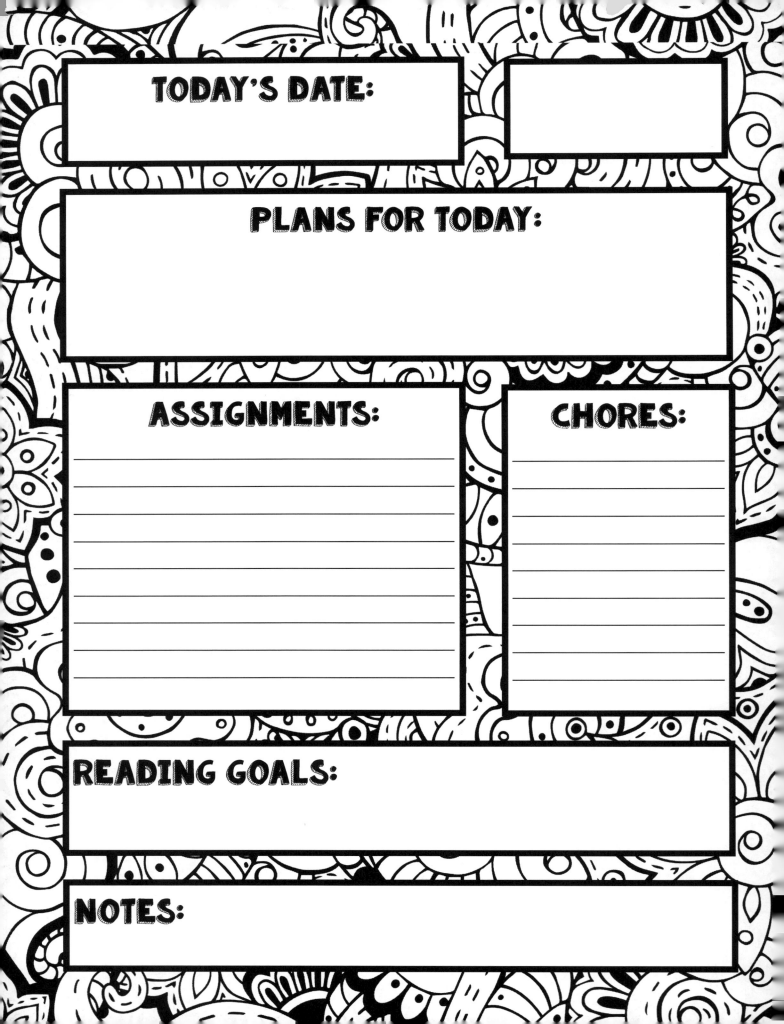

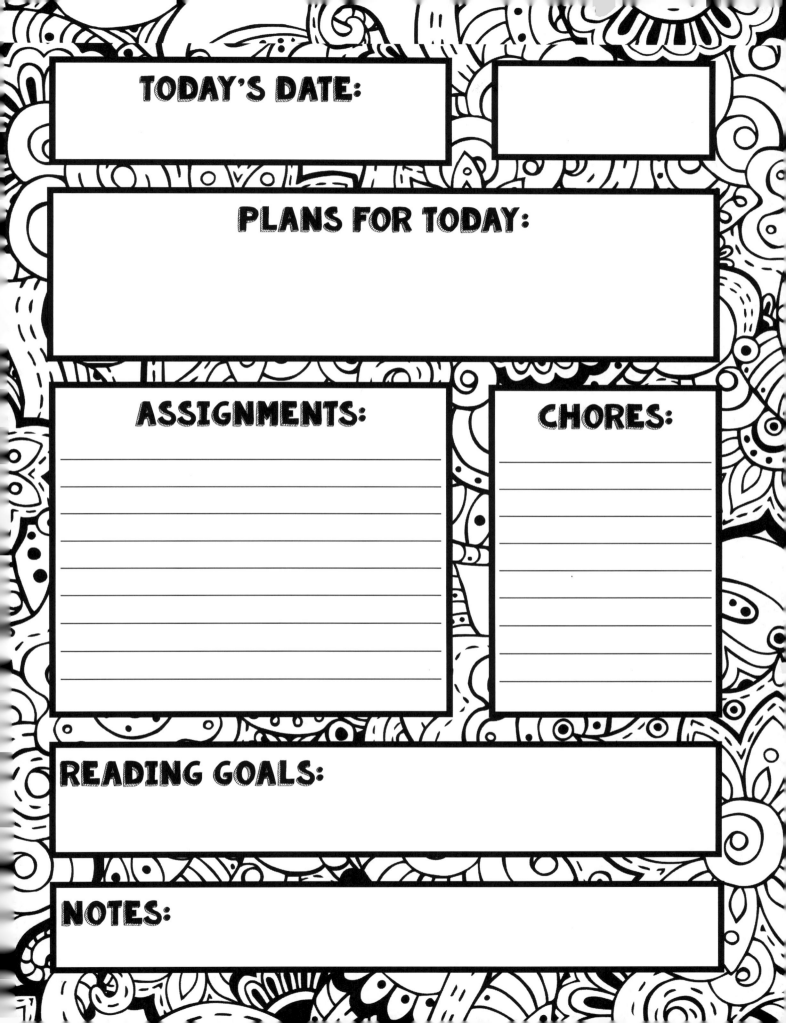

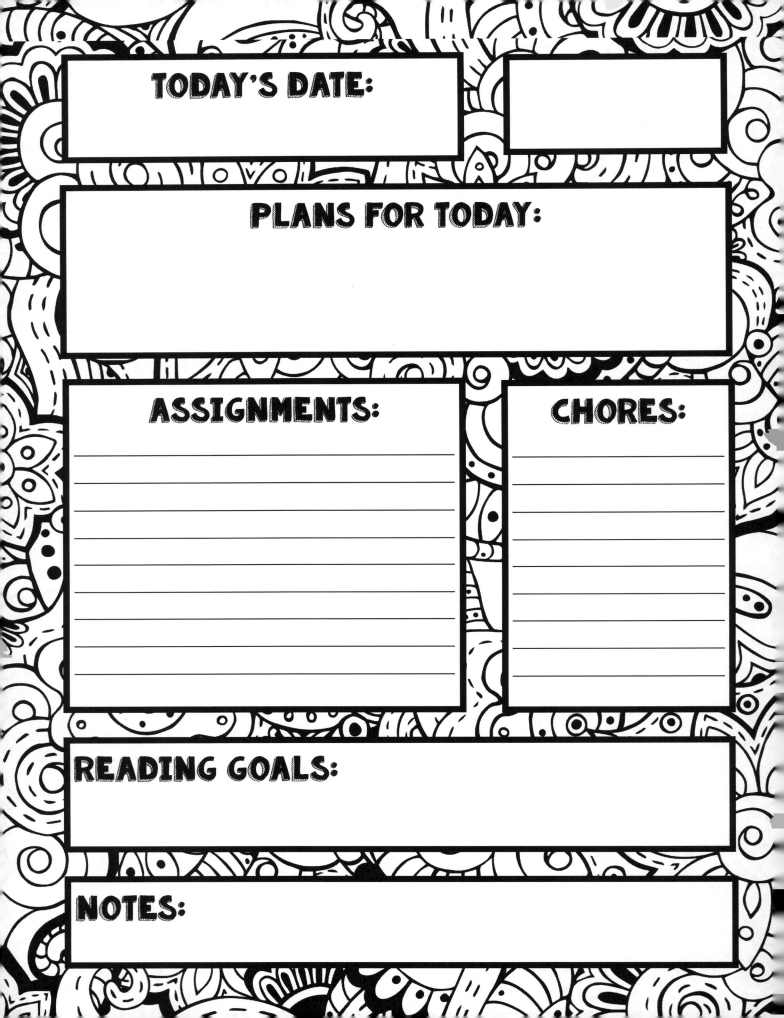

Plans & Perspective

"The home is the first and most effective place to learn the lessons of life: truth, honor, virtue, self control, the value of education, honest work, and the purpose and privilege of life." -McKay

My True Priorities

Long Term Goals

I Am Thankful For...

Checklist

Remember...

_____
_____
_____
_____
_____

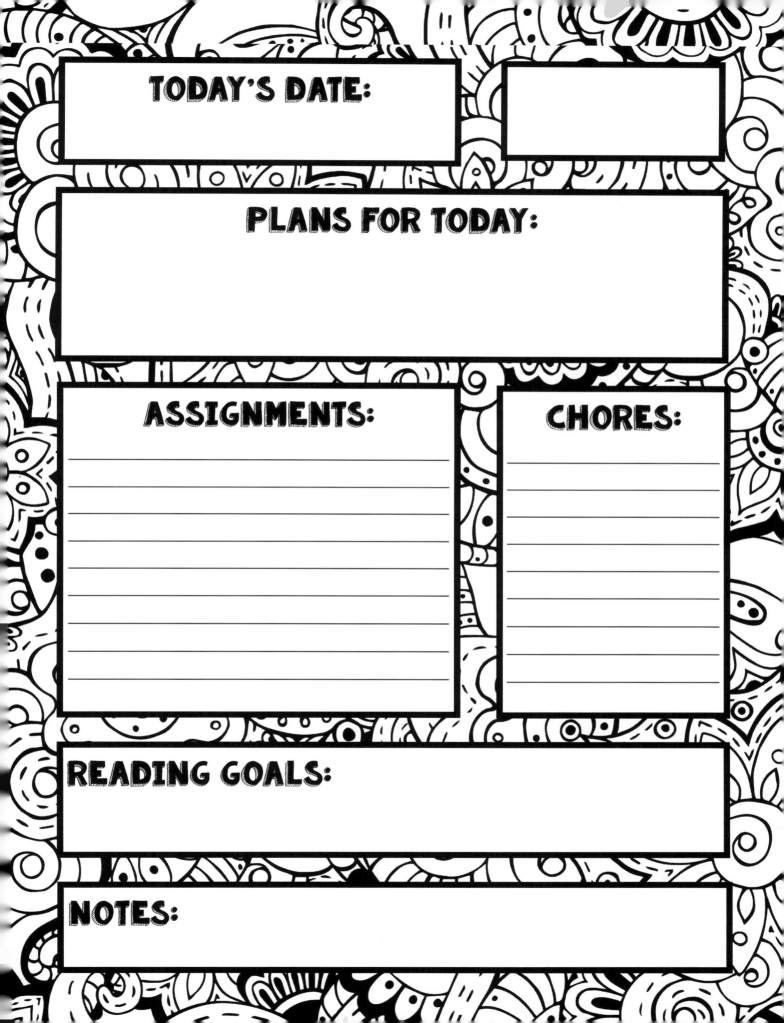

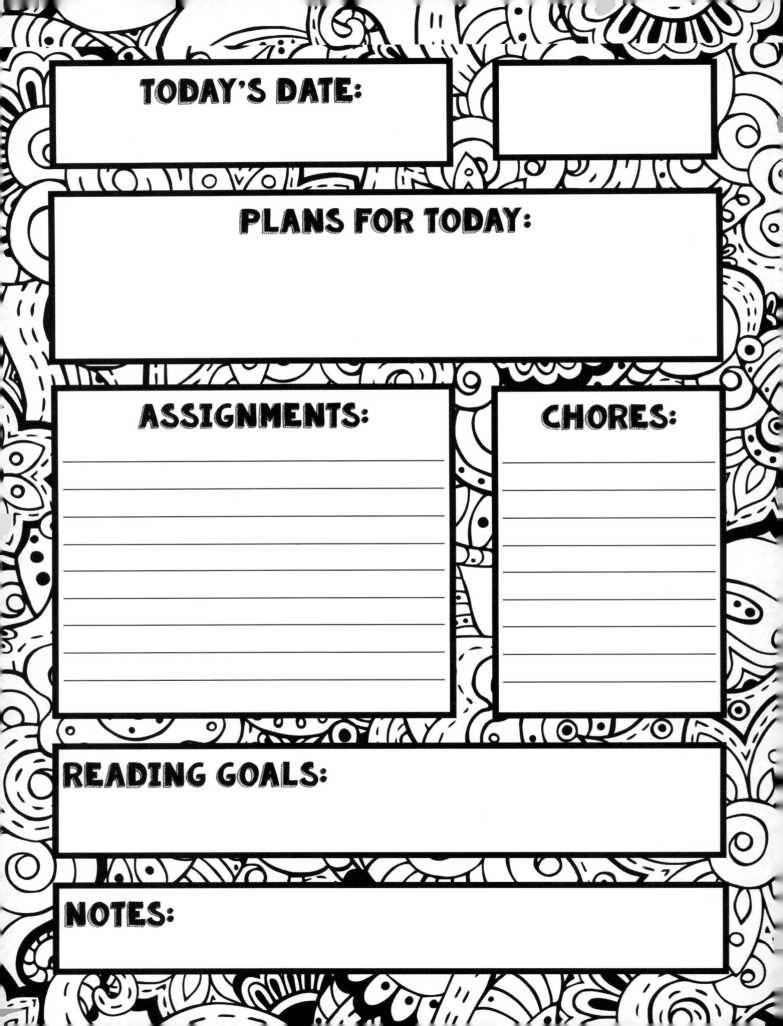

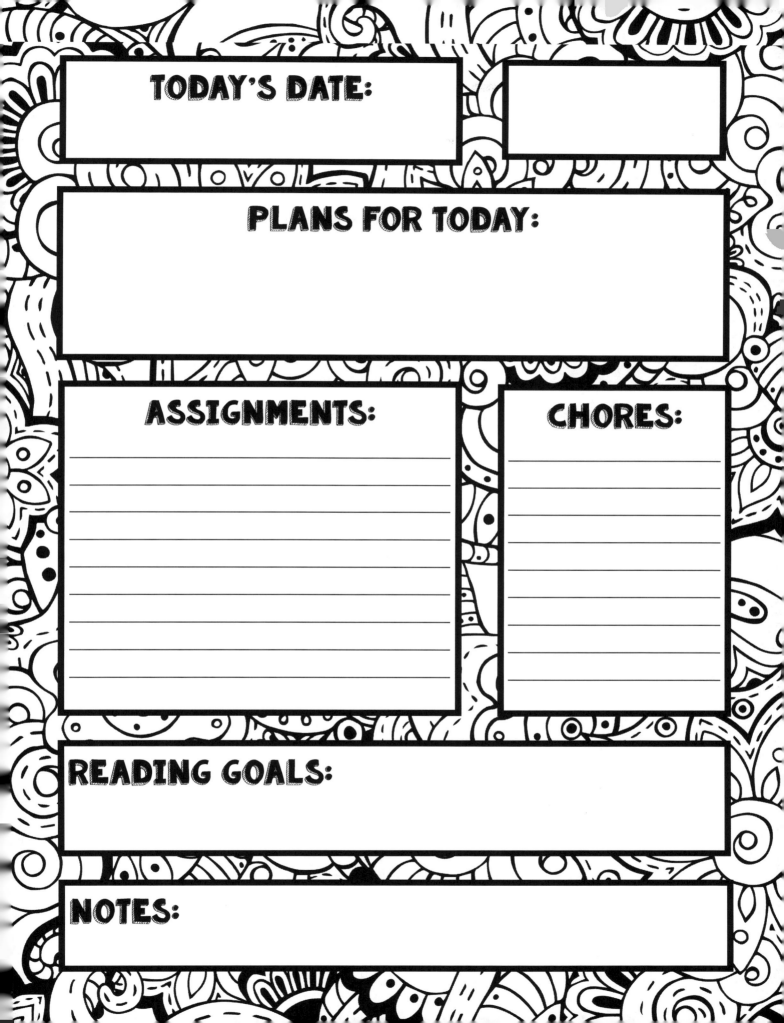

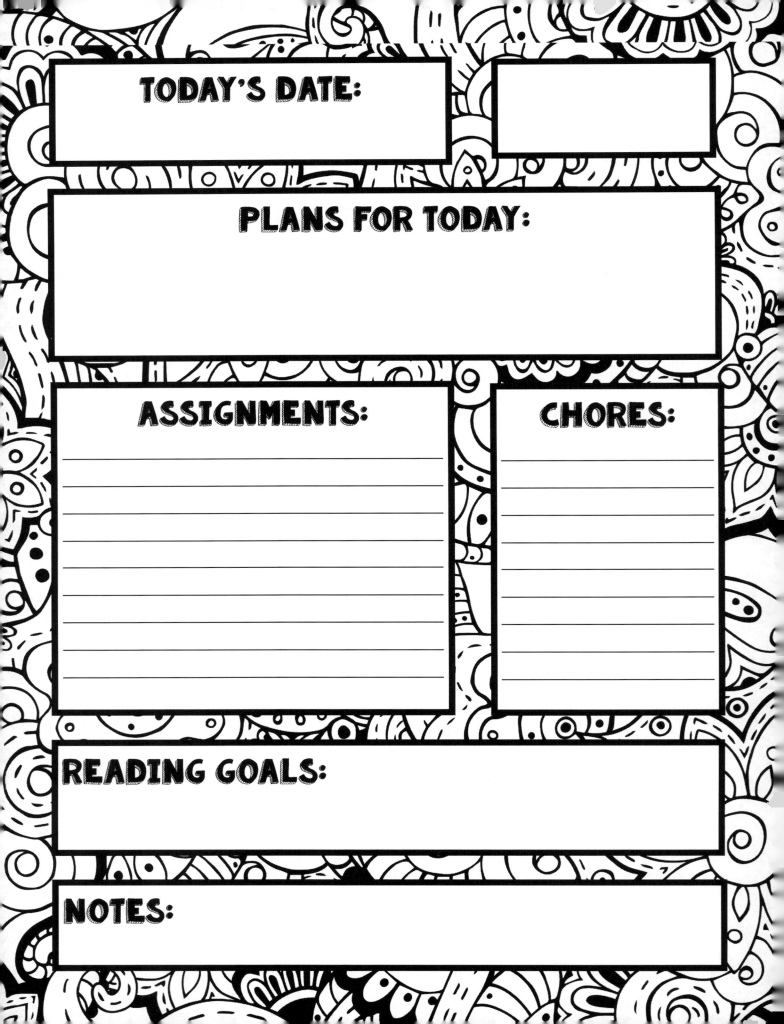

Plans & Perspective

"The home is the first and most effective place to learn the lessons of life: truth, honor, virtue, self control, the value of education, honest work, and the purpose and privilege of life." -McKay

My True Priorities

Long Term Goals

I Am Thankful For...

Checklist

Remember...

_____
_____
_____
_____
_____

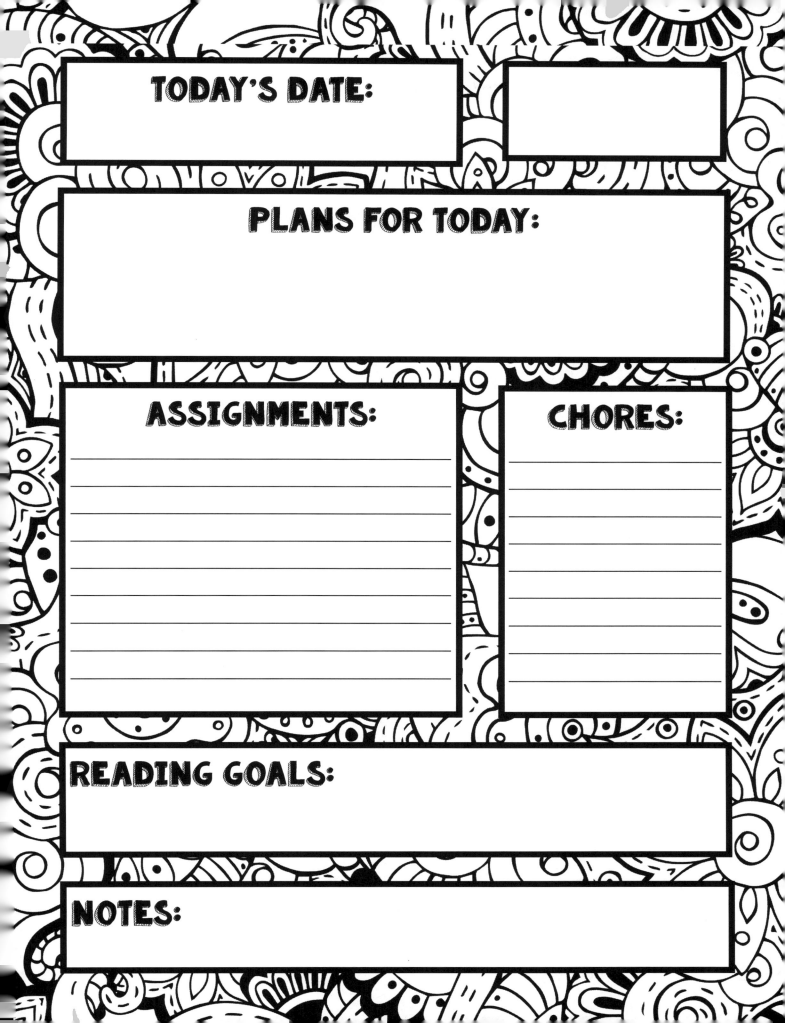

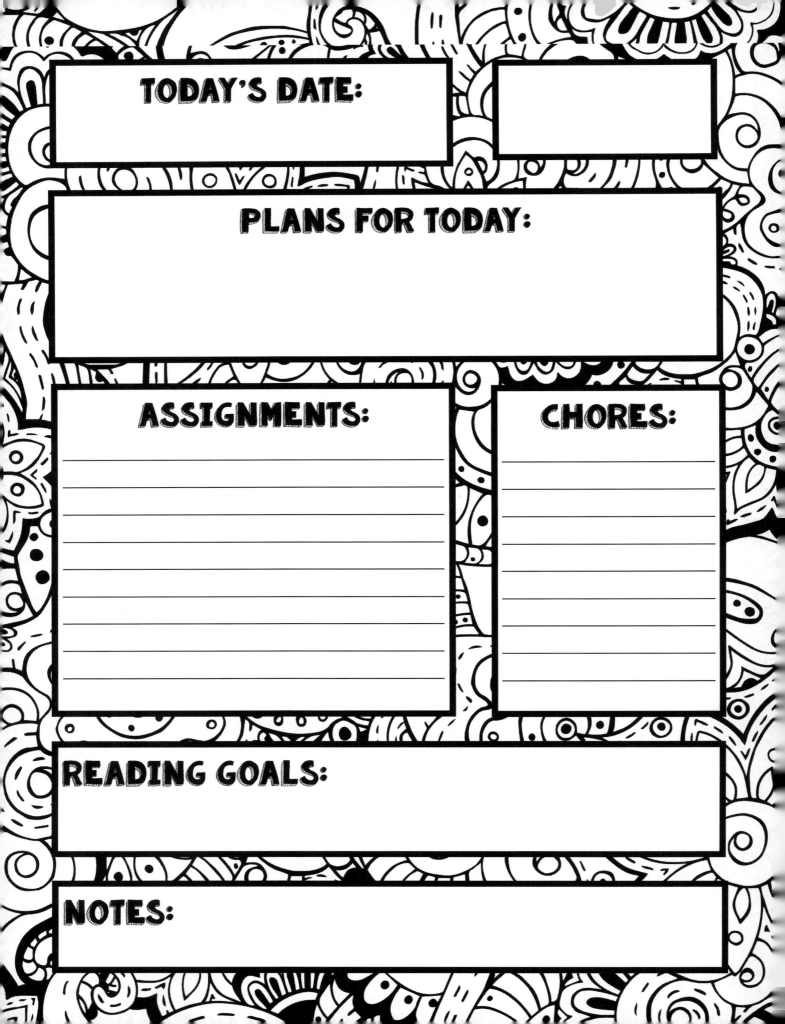

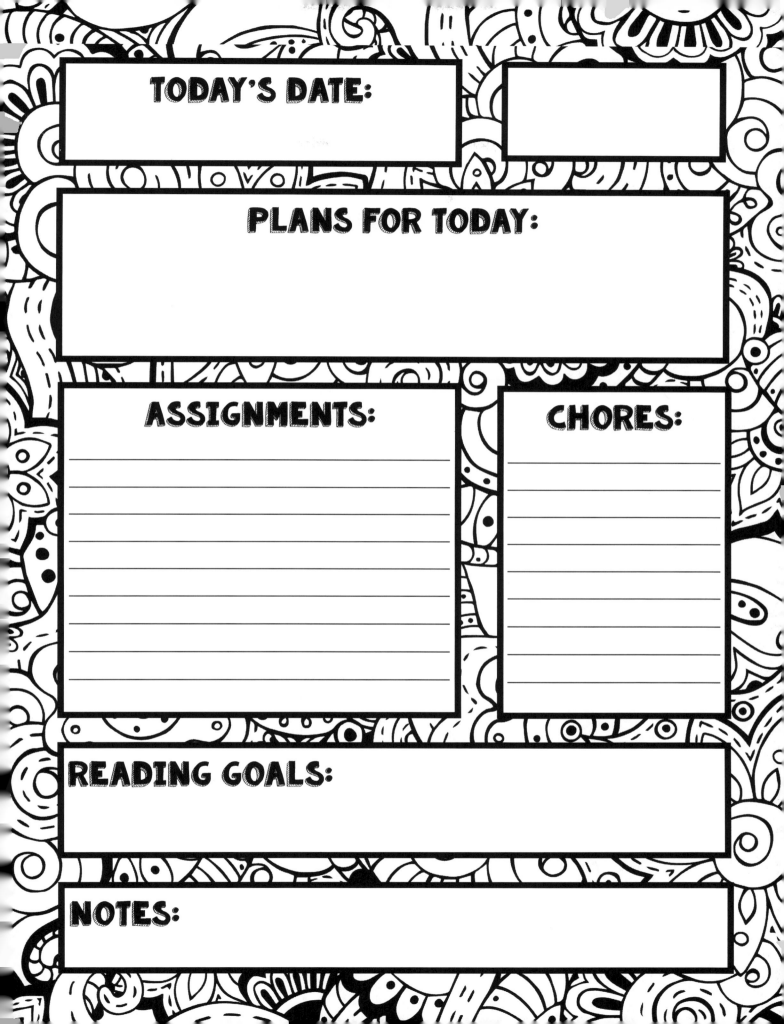

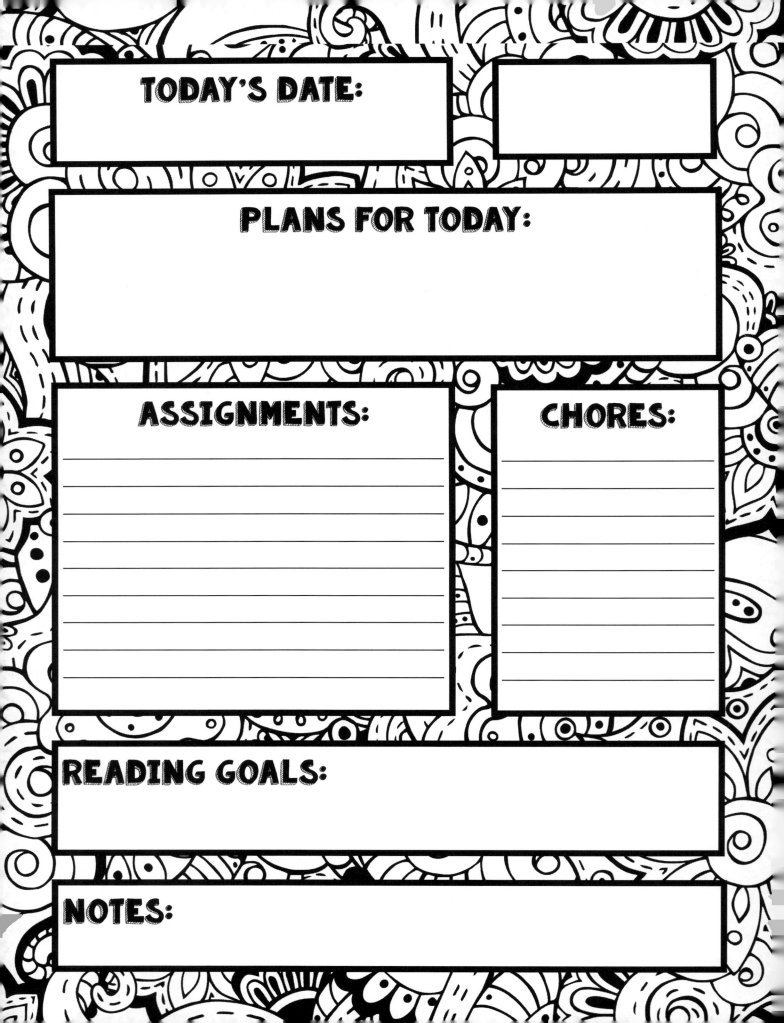

Plans & Perspective

"The home is the first and most effective place to learn the lessons of life: truth, honor, virtue, self control, the value of education, honest work, and the purpose and privilege of life." -McKay

My True Priorities

Long Term Goals

I Am Thankful For...

Checklist

Remember...

_____
_____
_____
_____
_____

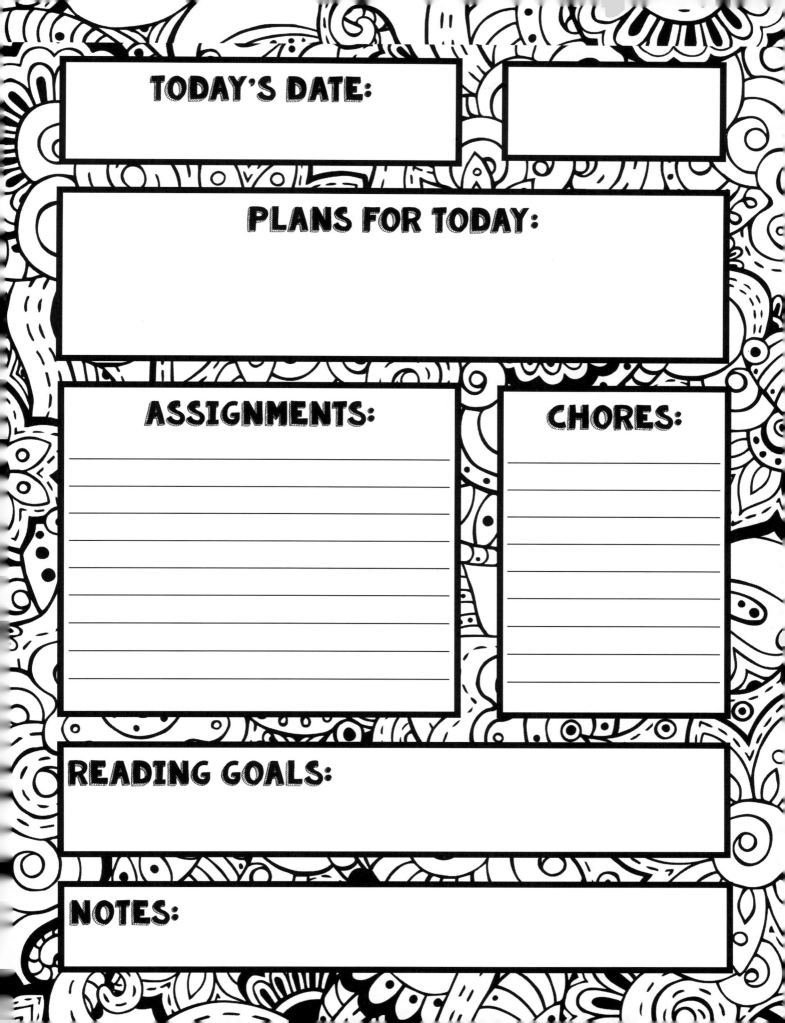

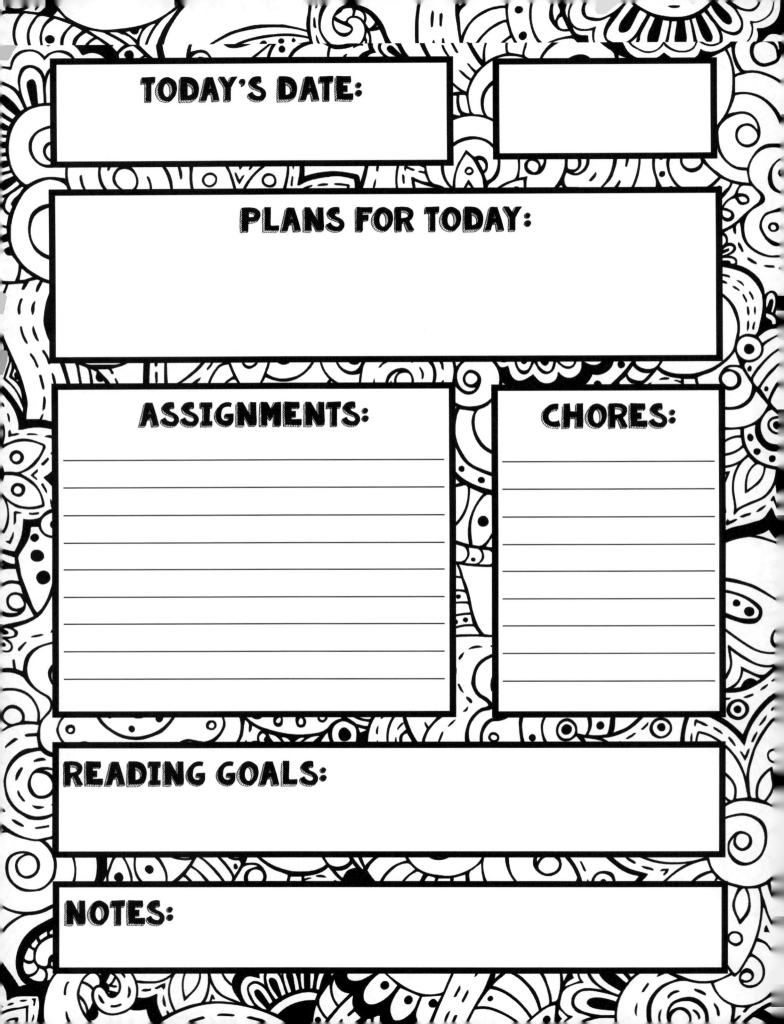

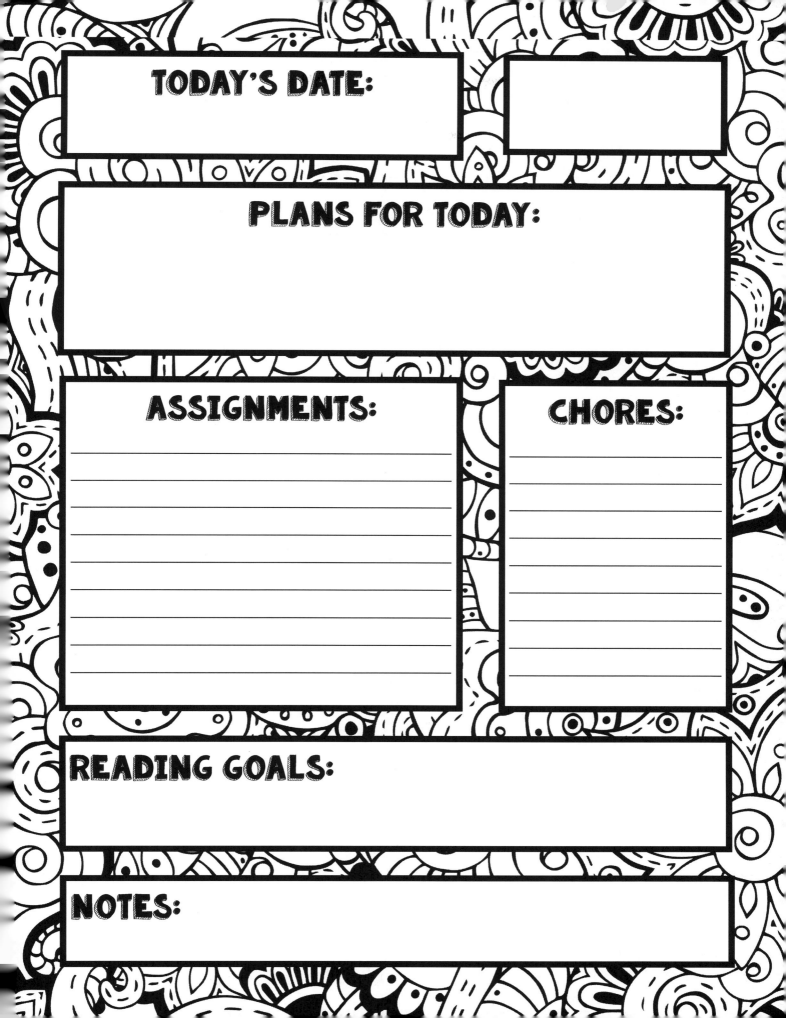

Plans & Perspective

"The home is the first and most effective place to learn the lessons of life: truth, honor, virtue, self control, the value of education, honest work, and the purpose and privilege of life." -McKay

My True Priorities

Long Term Goals

I Am Thankful For...

Checklist

Remember...

_____
_____
_____
_____
_____

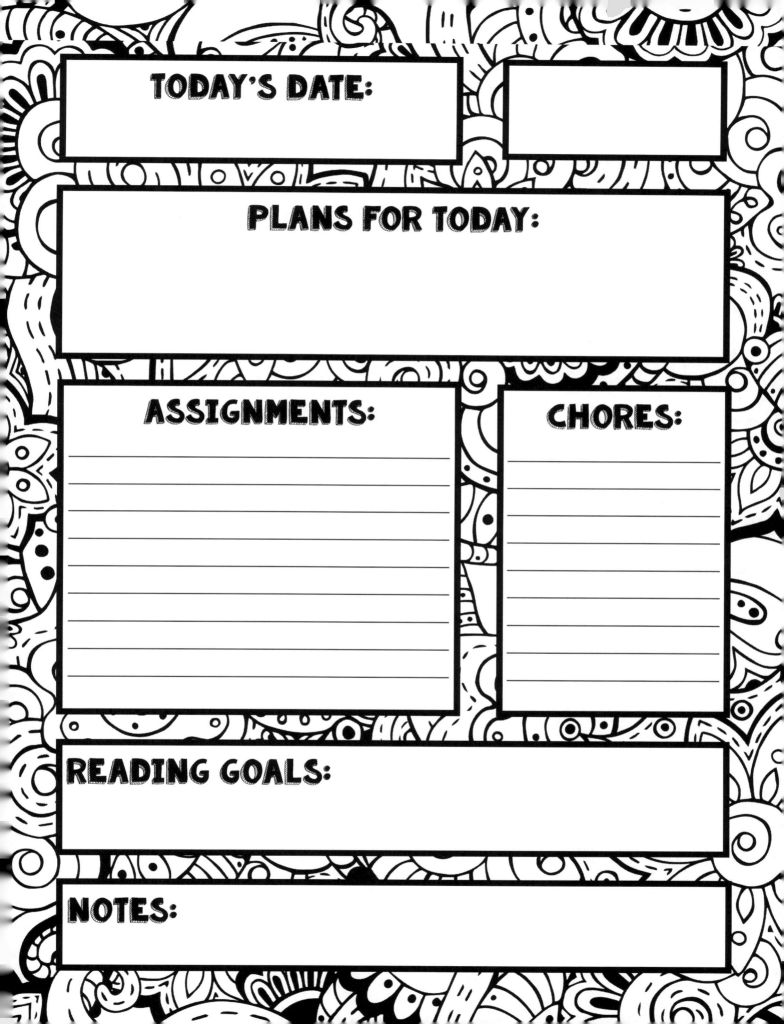

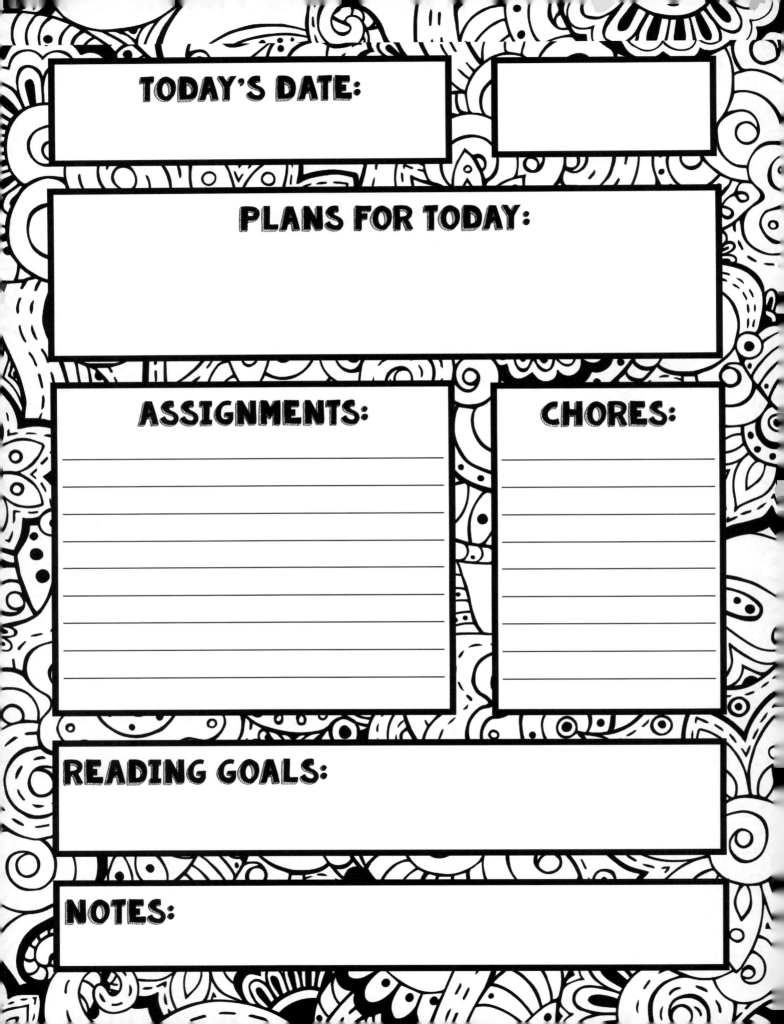

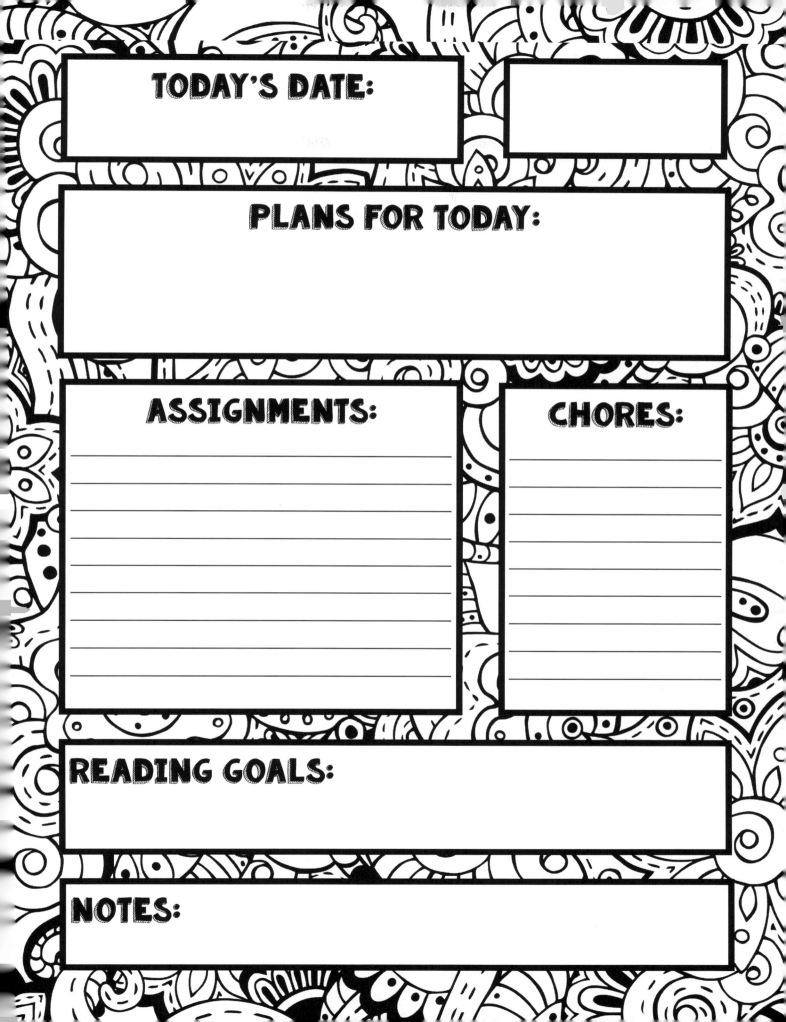

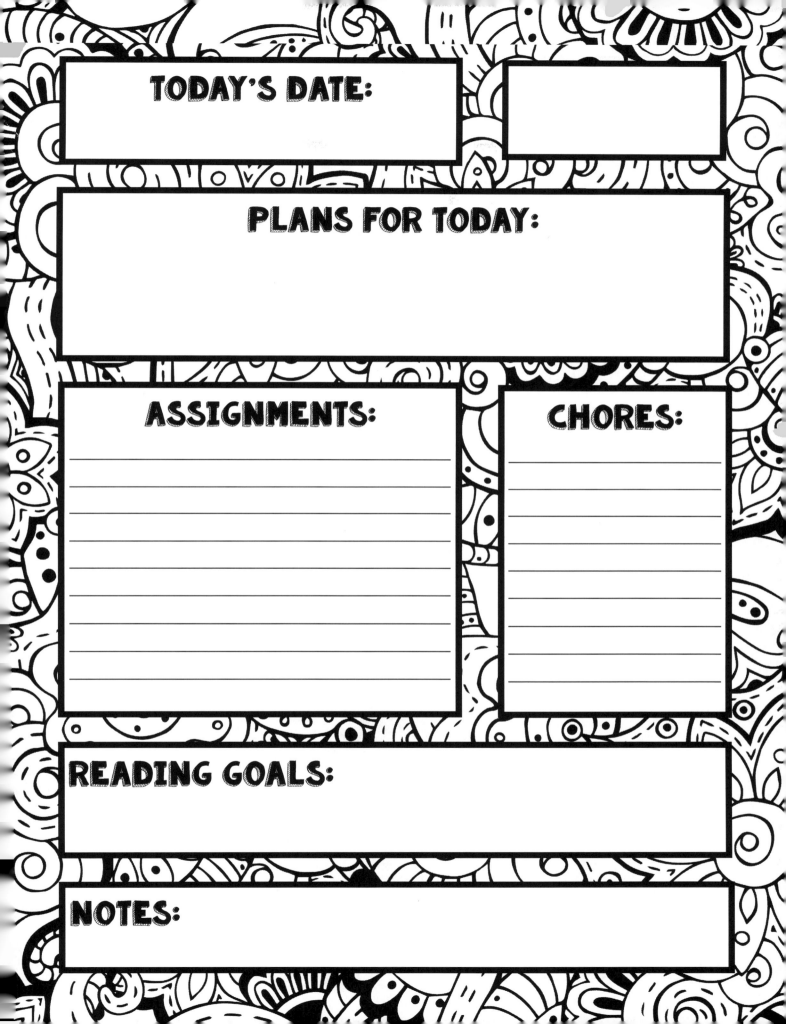

Plans & Perspective

"The home is the first and most effective place to learn the lessons of life: truth, honor, virtue, self control, the value of education, honest work, and the purpose and privilege of life." -McKay

My True Priorities

Long Term Goals

I Am Thankful For...

Checklist

Remember...

___
___
___
___
___

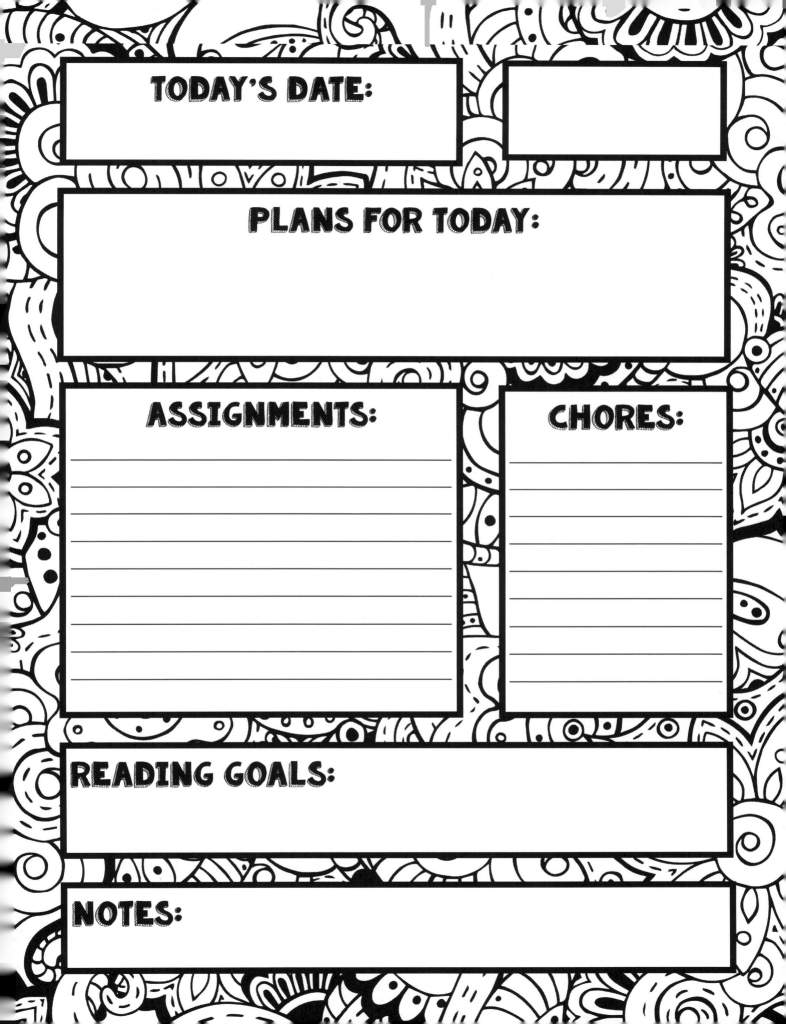

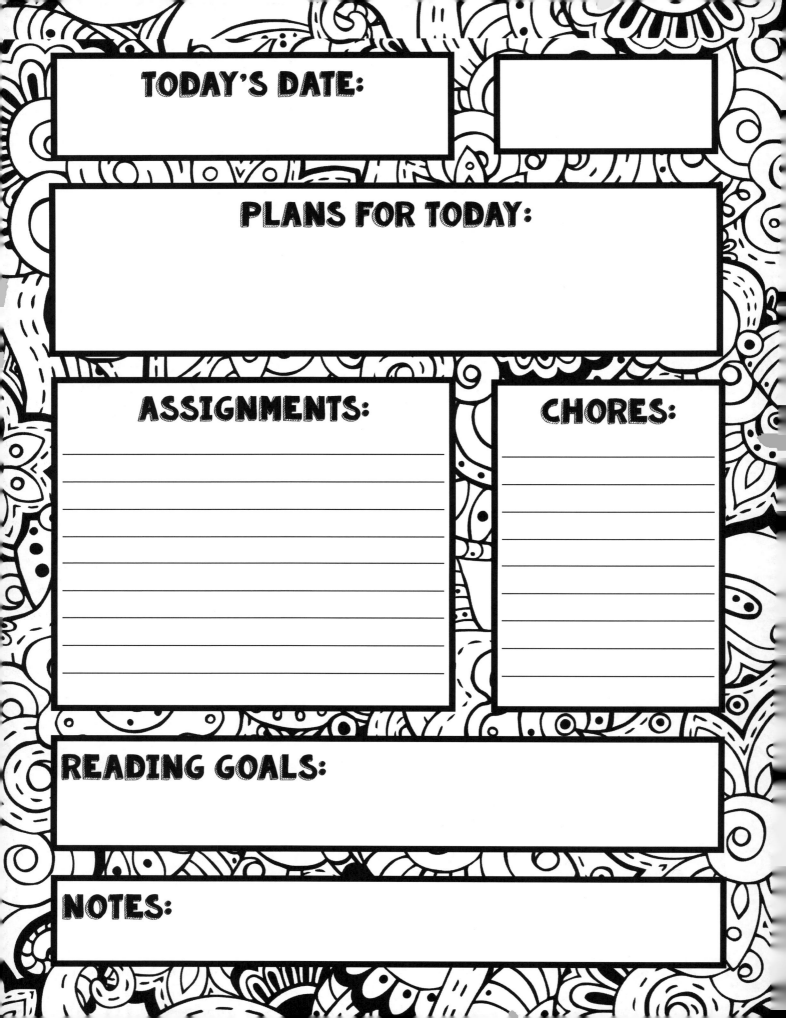

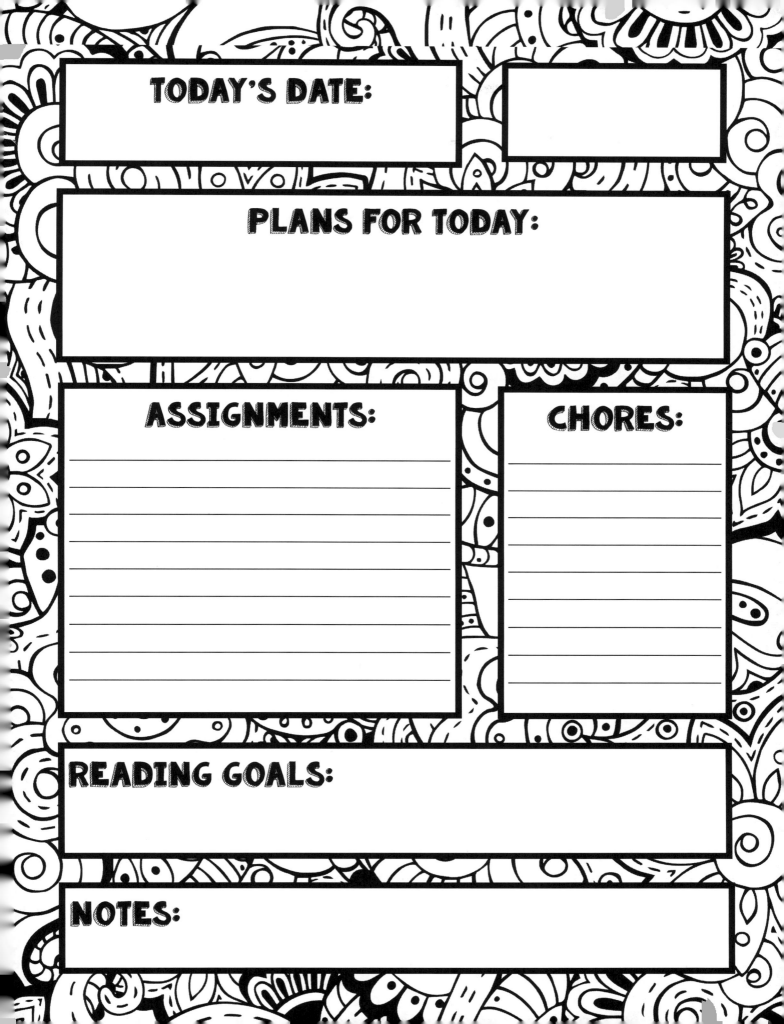

Plans & Perspective

"The home is the first and most effective place to learn the lessons of life: truth, honor, virtue, self control, the value of education, honest work, and the purpose and privilege of life." -McKay

My True Priorities

Long Term Goals

I Am Thankful For...

Checklist

Remember...

_____
_____
_____
_____
_____

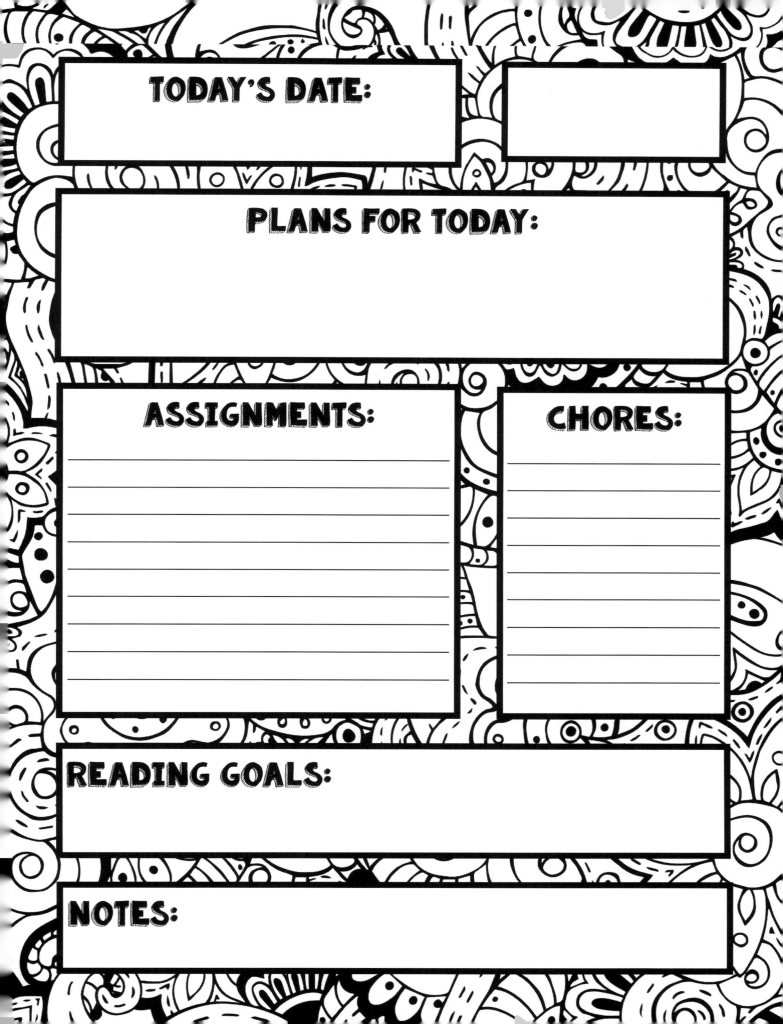

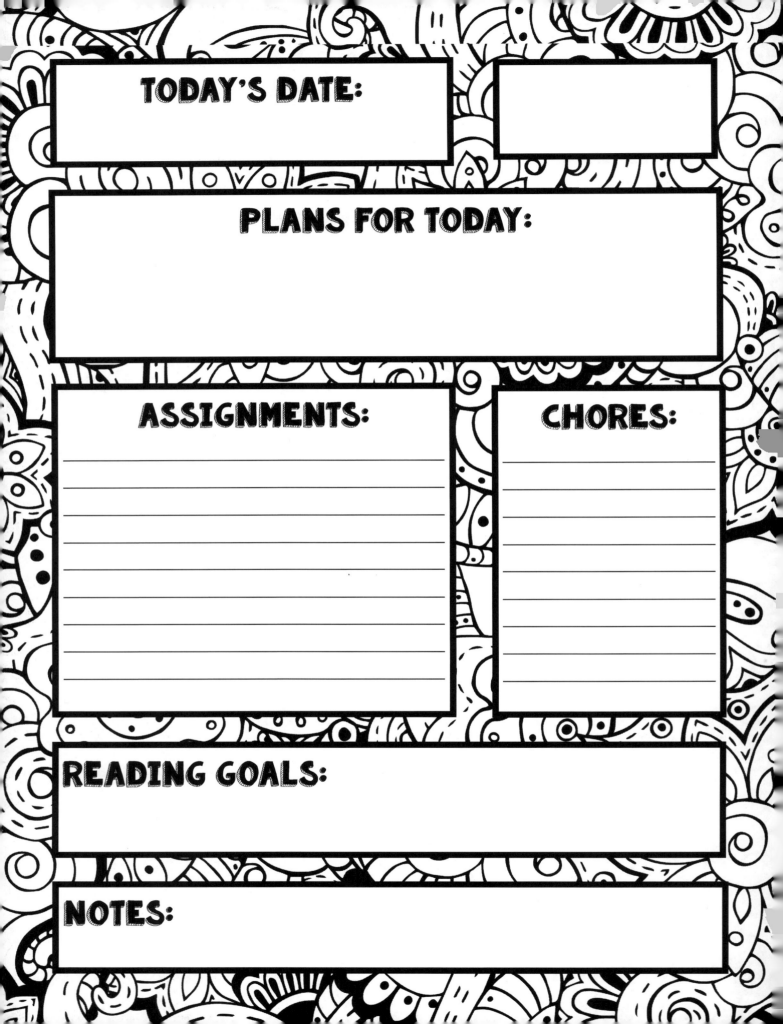

TODAY'S DATE:

PLANS FOR TODAY:

ASSIGNMENTS:

CHORES:

READING GOALS:

NOTES:

Plans & Perspective

"The home is the first and most effective place to learn the lessons of life: truth, honor, virtue, self control, the value of education, honest work, and the purpose and privilege of life." -McKay

My True Priorities

Long Term Goals

I Am Thankful For...

Checklist

Remember...

_____
_____
_____
_____
_____

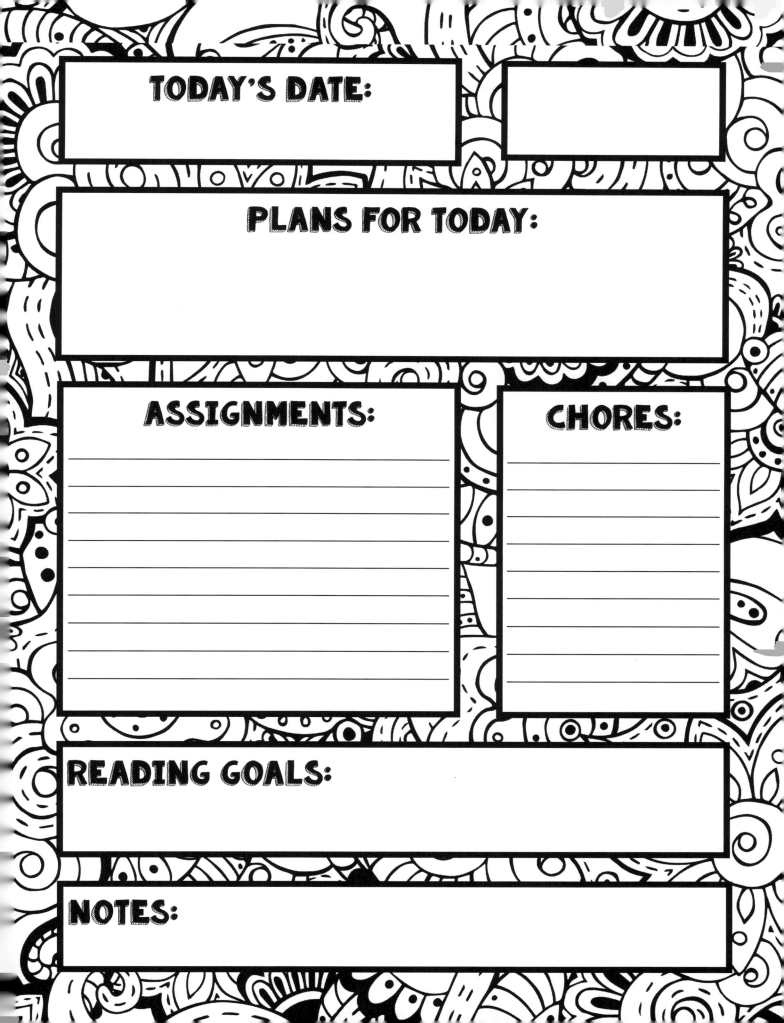

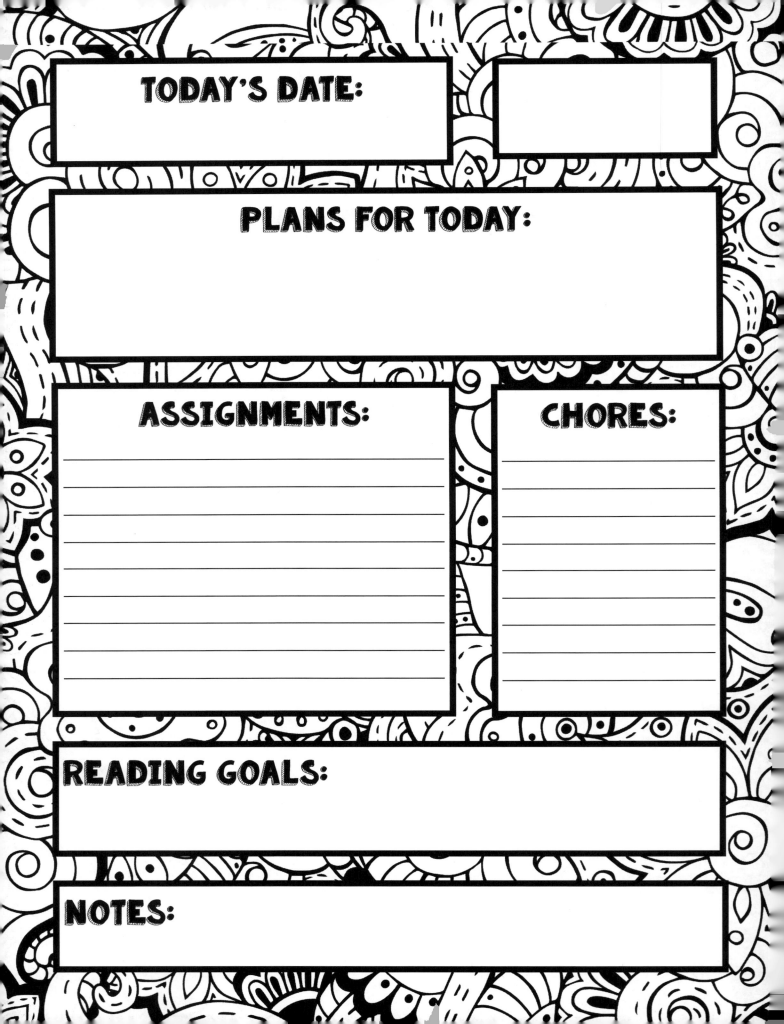

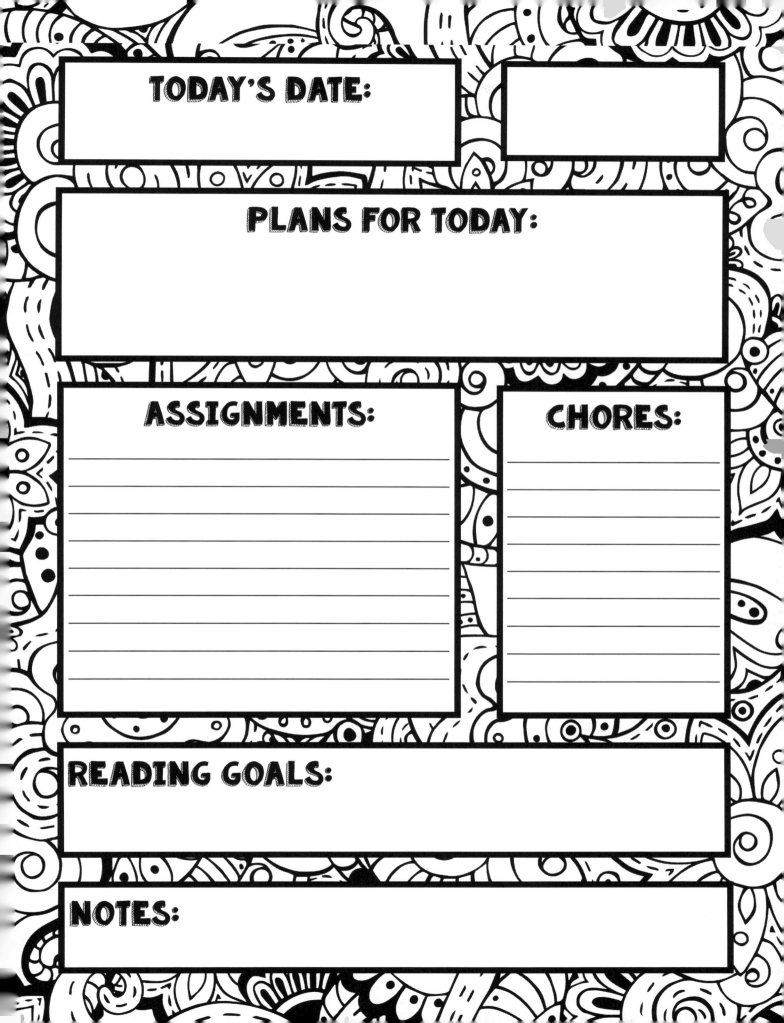

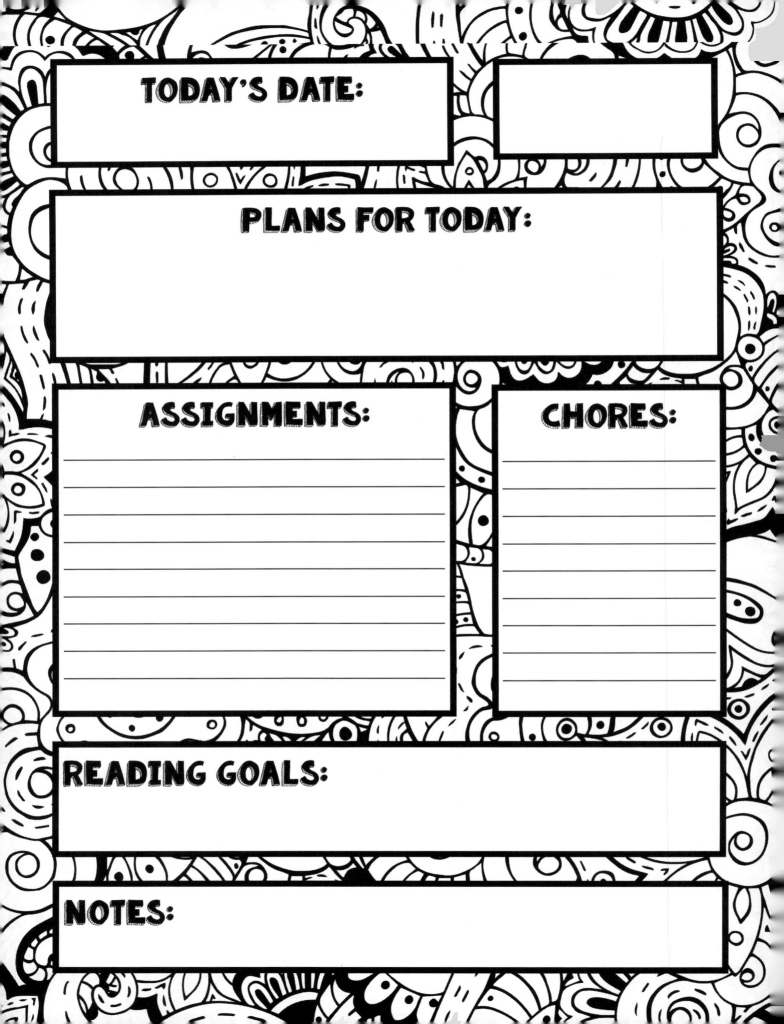

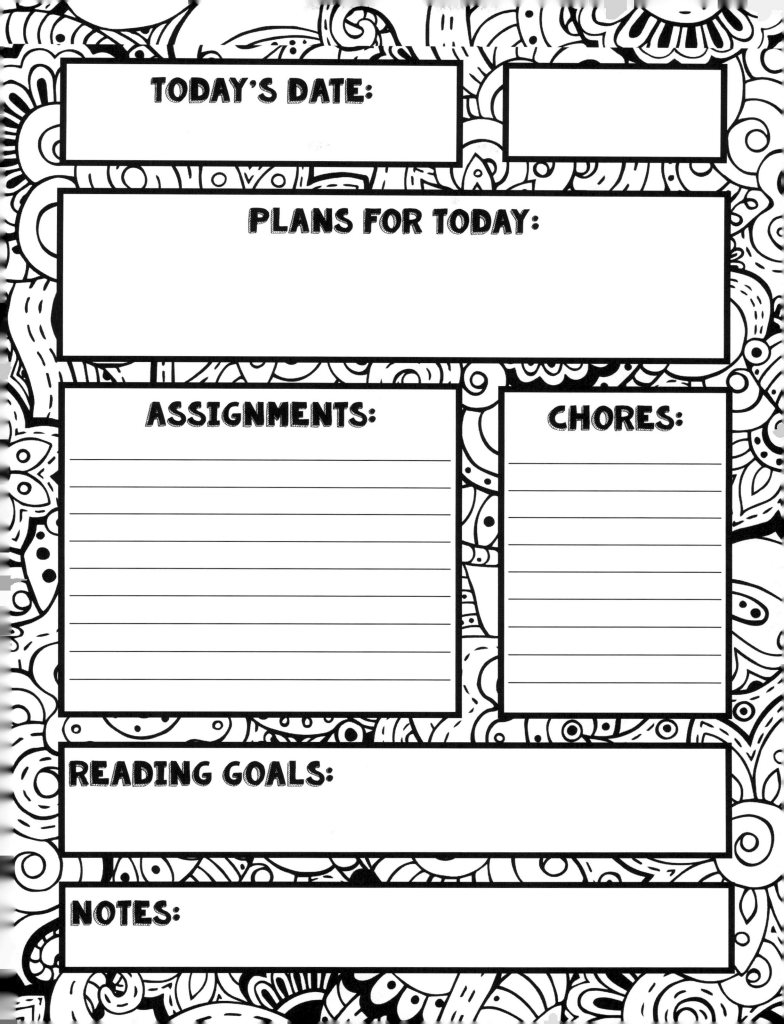

Plans & Perspective

"The home is the first and most effective place to learn the lessons of life: truth, honor, virtue, self control, the value of education, honest work, and the purpose and privilege of life." -McKay

My True Priorities

Long Term Goals

I Am Thankful For...

Checklist

Remember...

_____
_____
_____
_____
_____

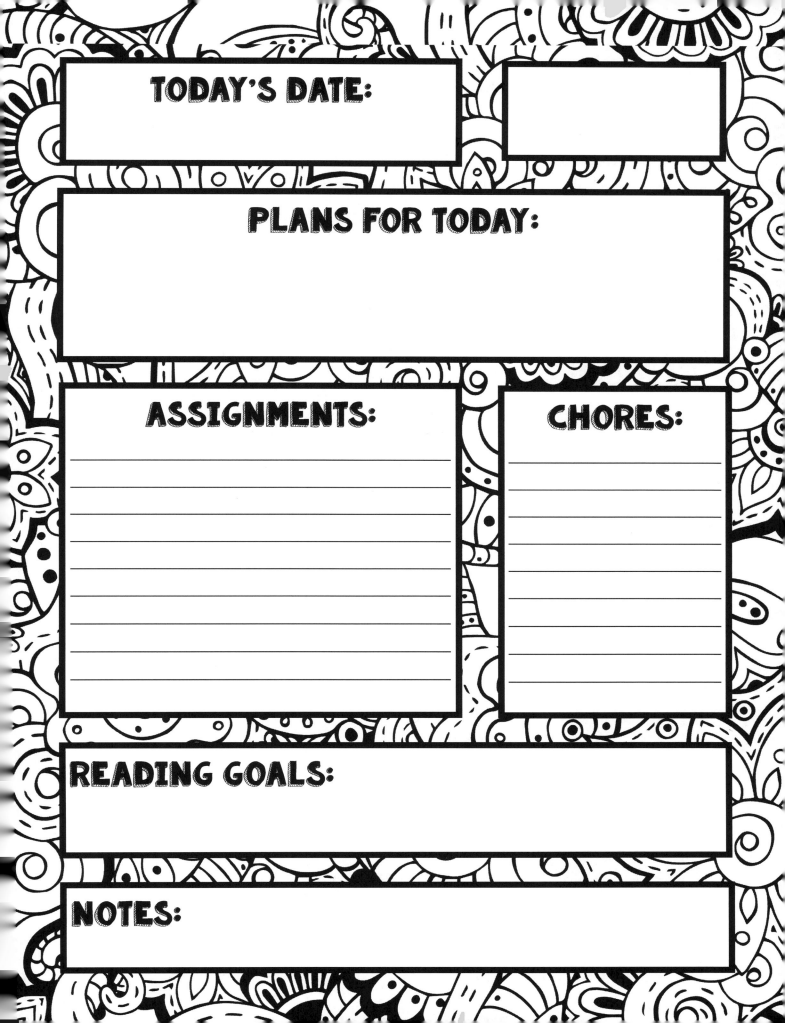

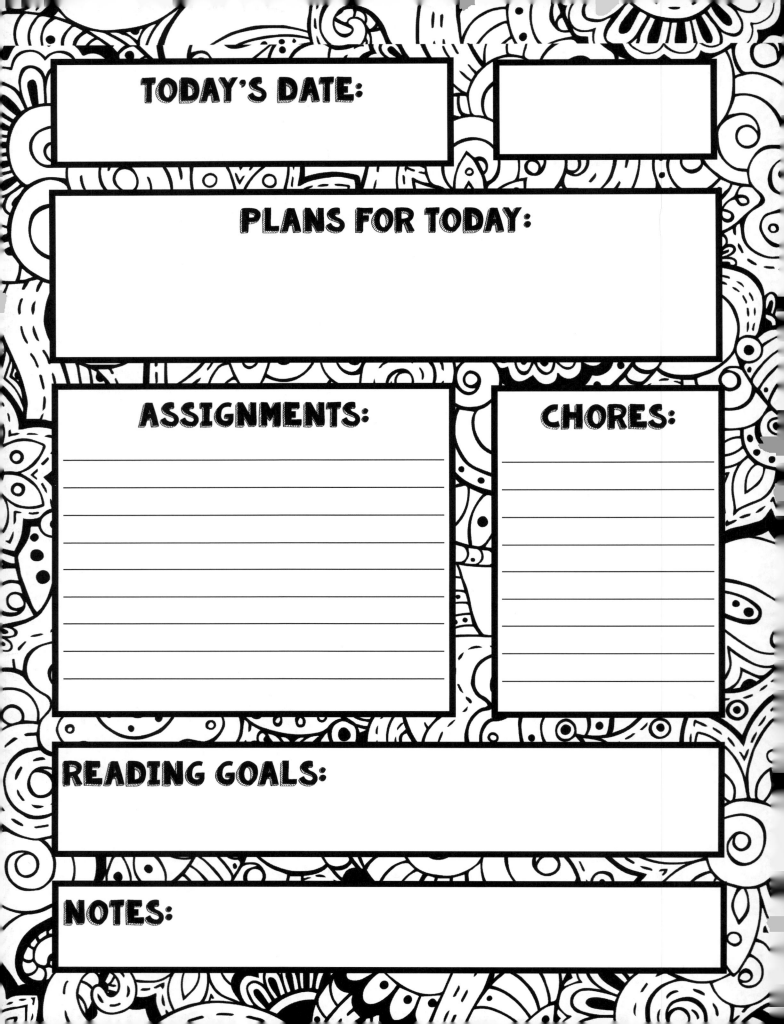

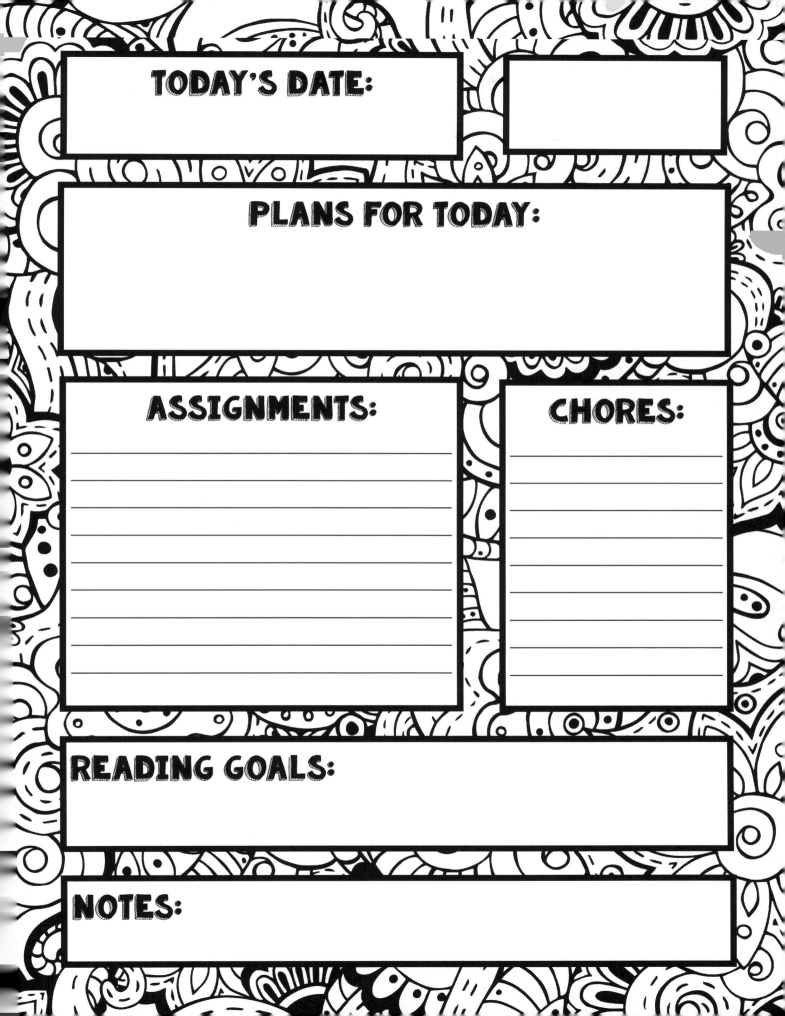

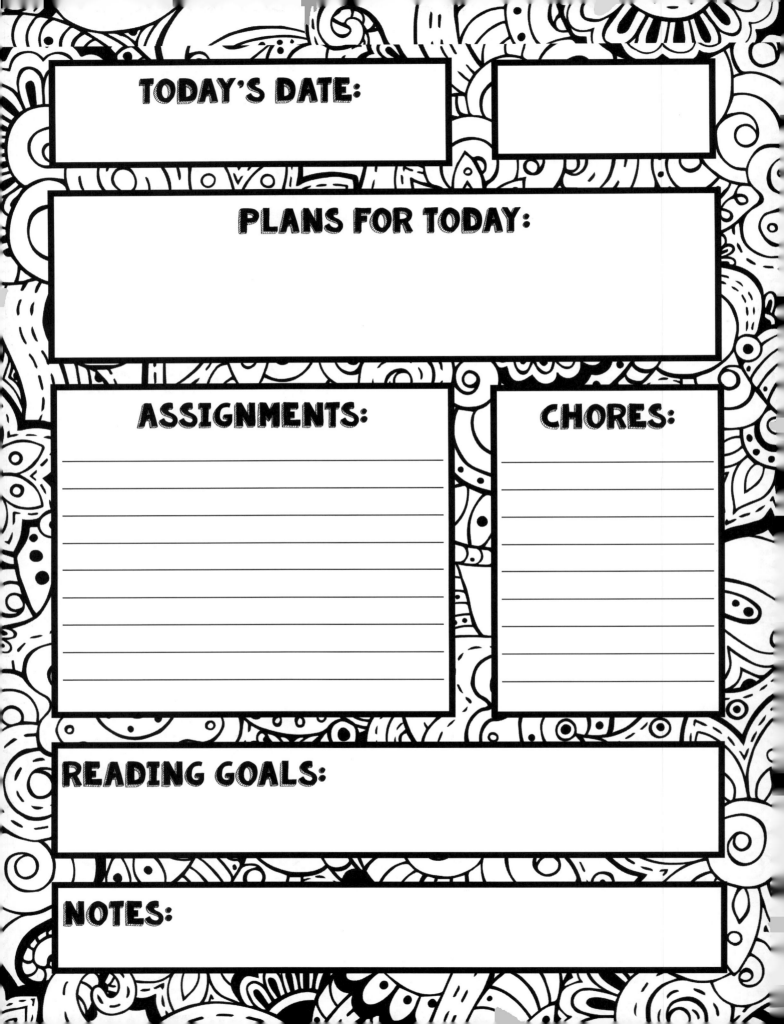

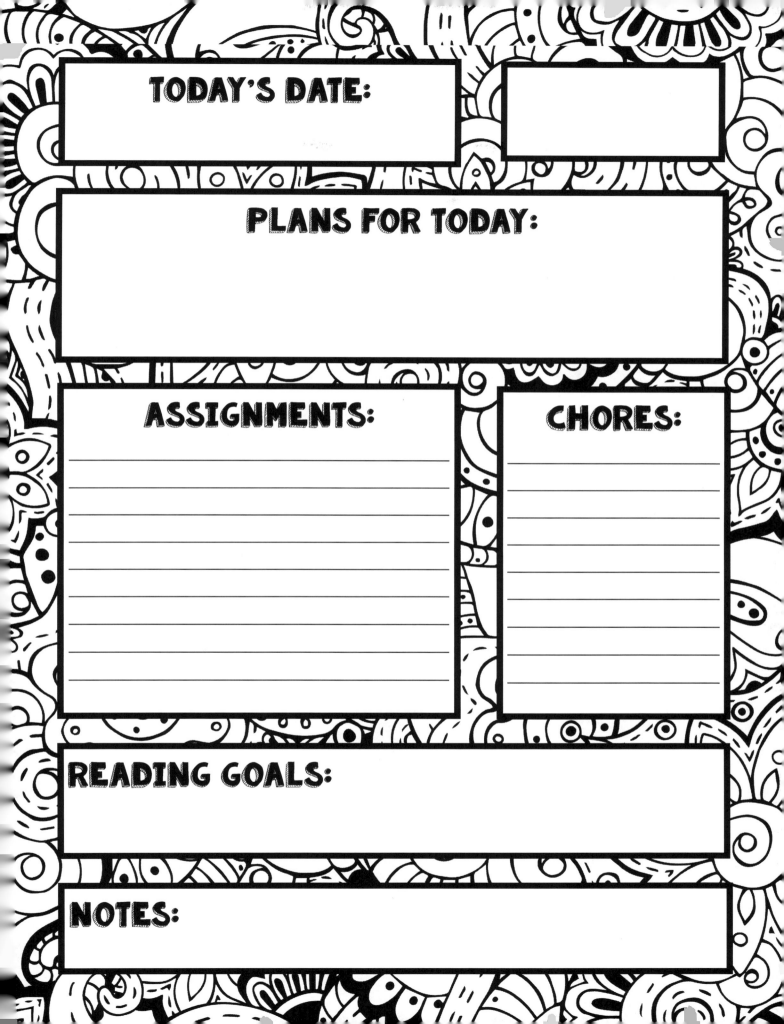

Plans & Perspective

"The home is the first and most effective place to learn the lessons of life: truth, honor, virtue, self control, the value of education, honest work, and the purpose and privilege of life." -McKay

My True Priorities

Long Term Goals

I Am Thankful For...

Checklist

Remember...

_____
_____
_____
_____
_____

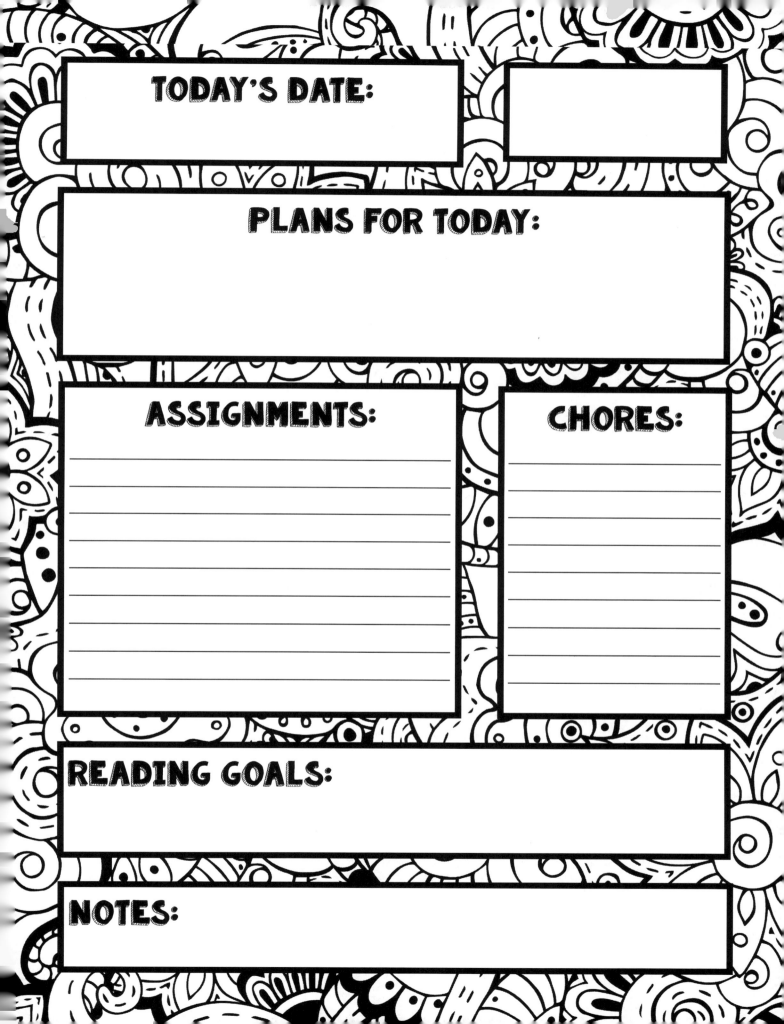

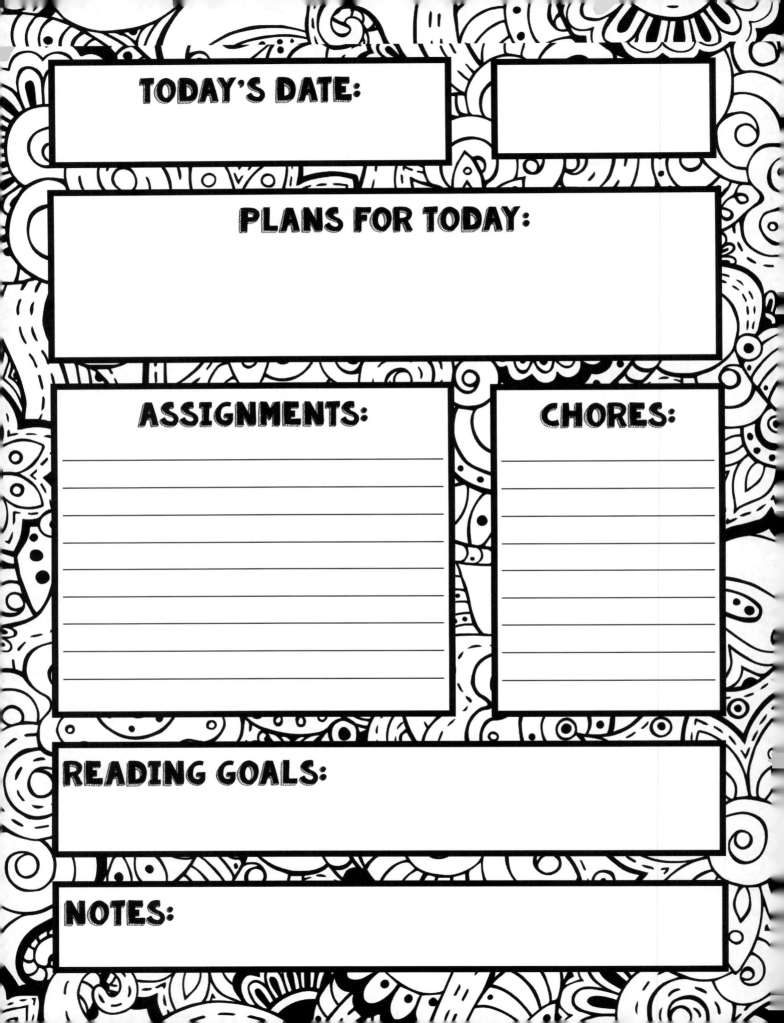

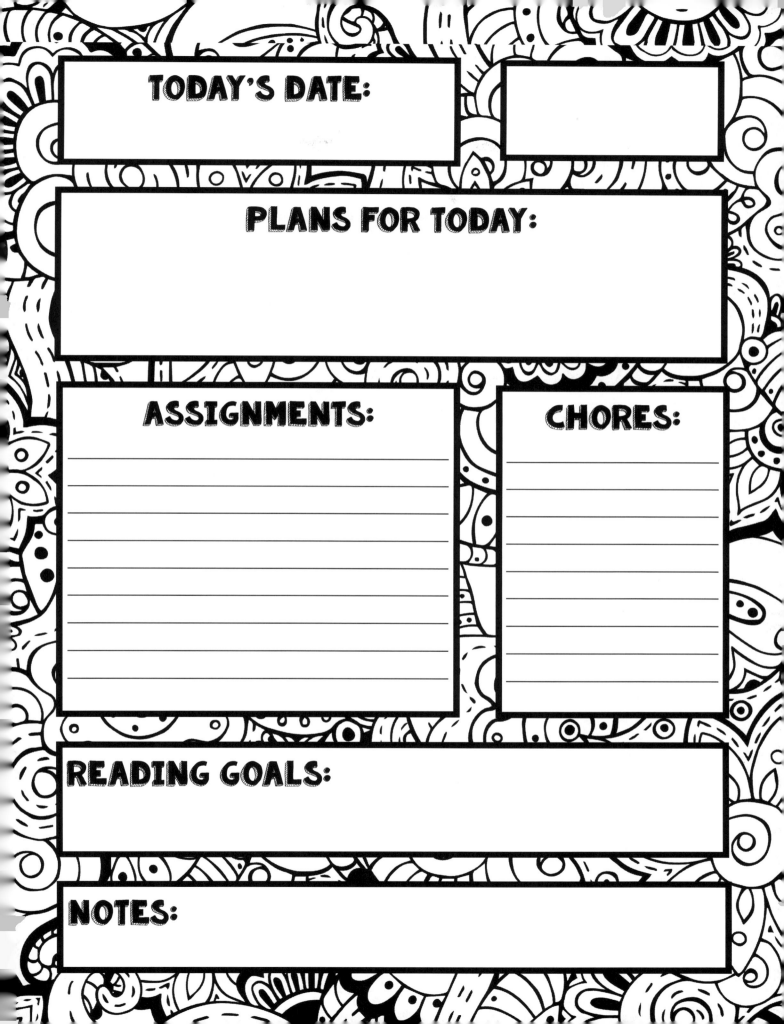

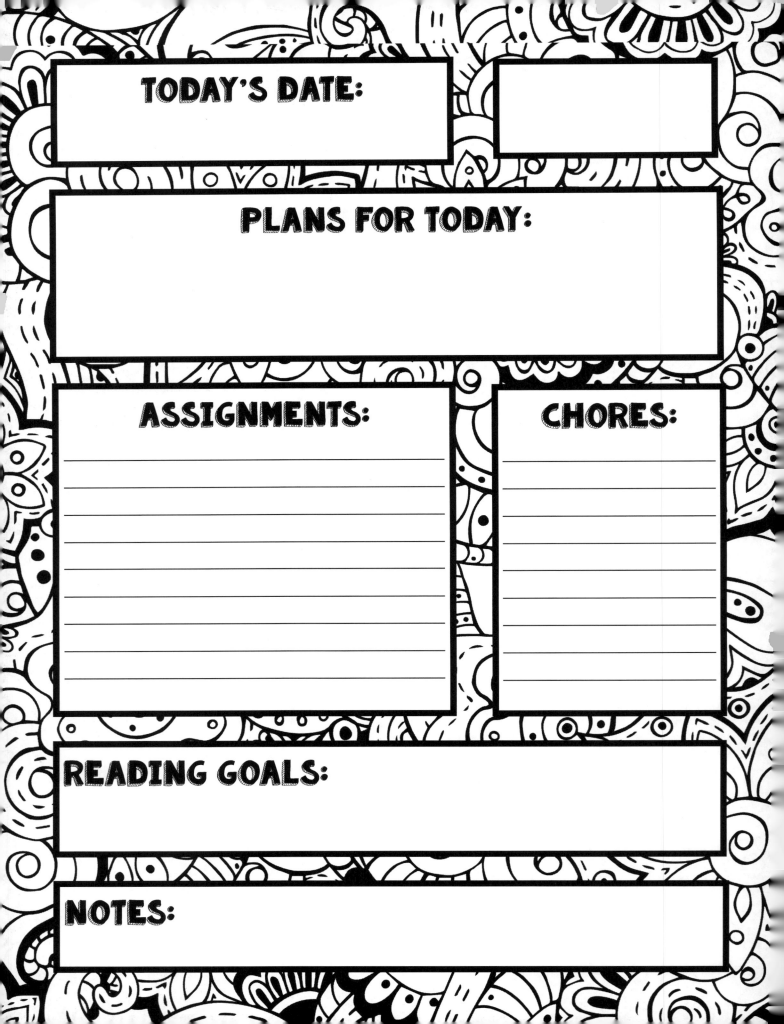

Plans & Perspective

"The home is the first and most effective place to learn the lessons of life: truth, honor, virtue, self control, the value of education, honest work, and the purpose and privilege of life." -McKay

My True Priorities

Long Term Goals

I Am Thankful For...

Checklist

Remember...

_____
_____
_____
_____
_____

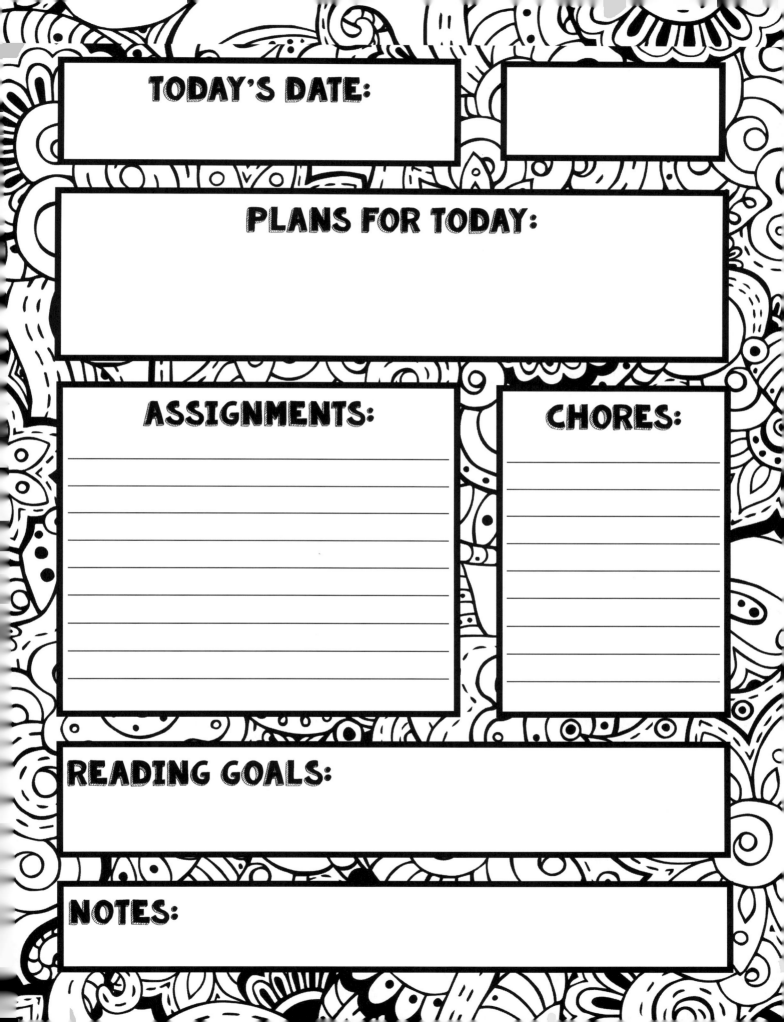

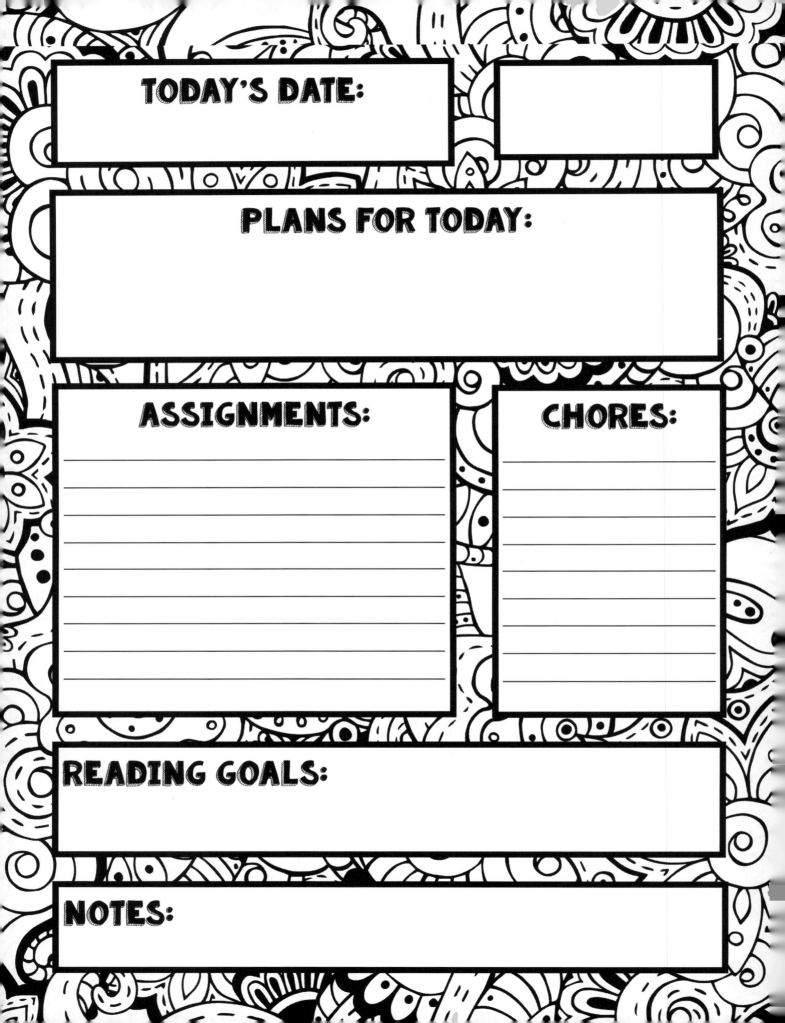

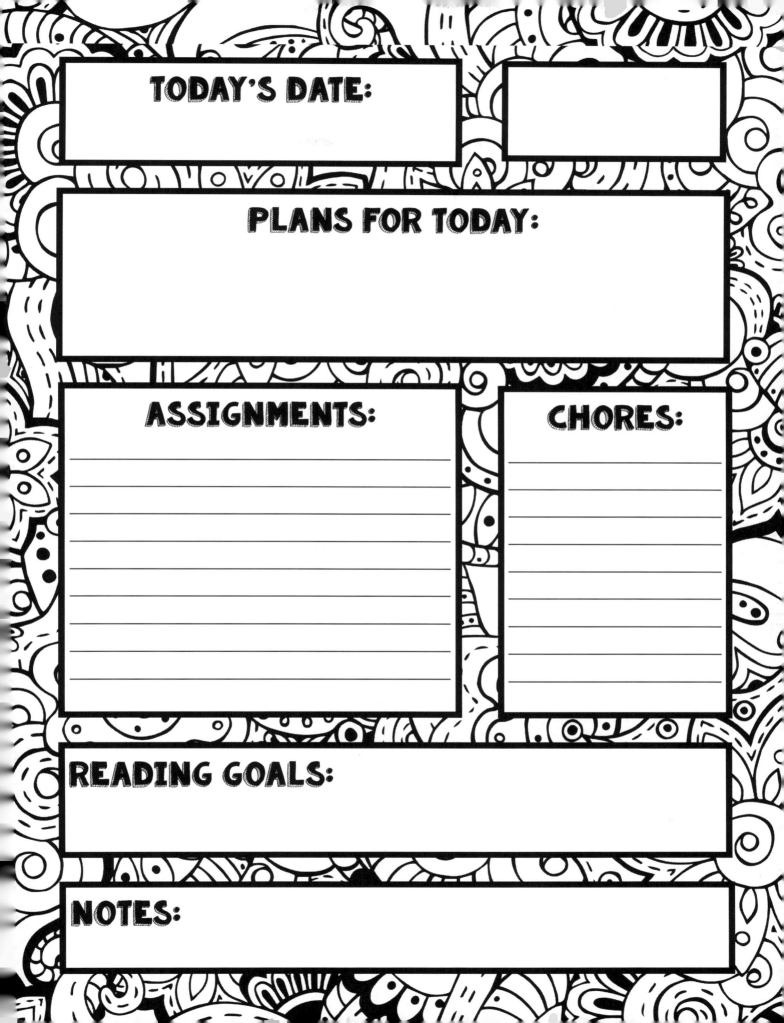

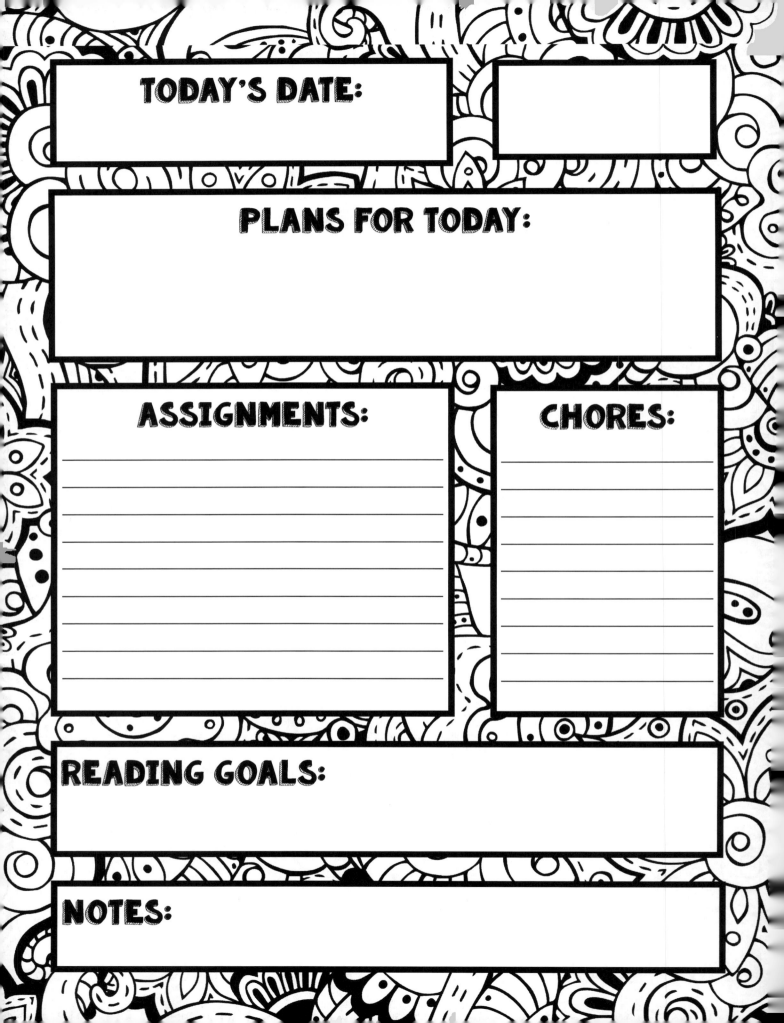

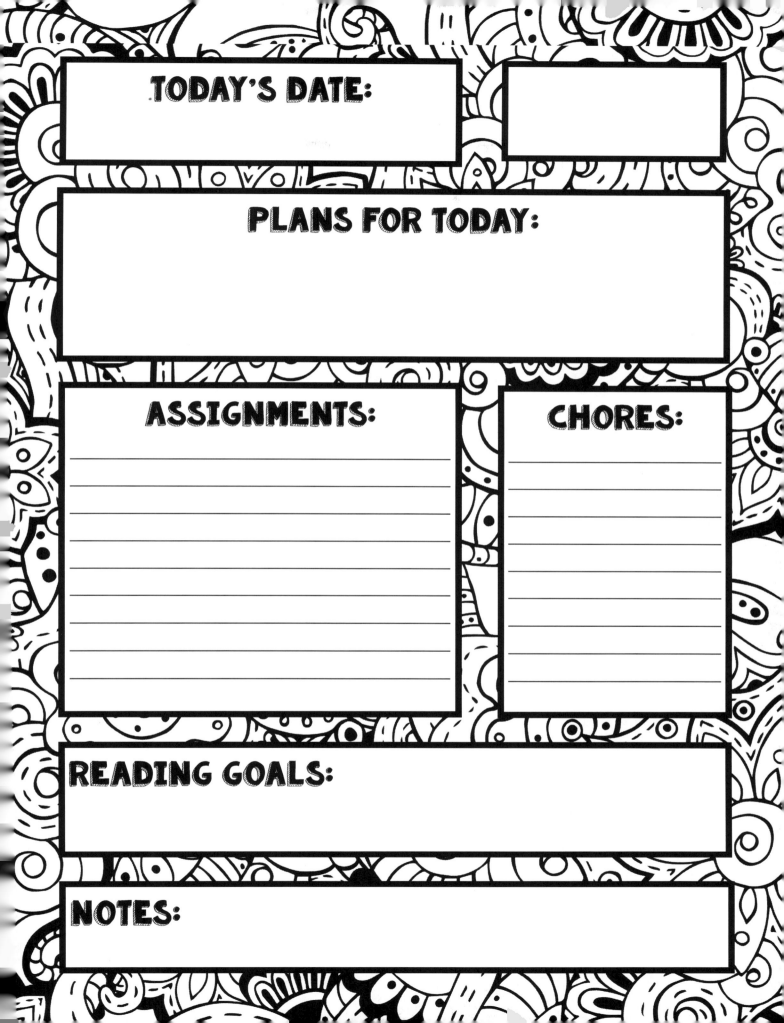

Plans & Perspective

"The home is the first and most effective place to learn the lessons of life: truth, honor, virtue, self control, the value of education, honest work, and the purpose and privilege of life." -McKay

My True Priorities

Long Term Goals

I Am Thankful For...

Checklist

Remember...

_____
_____
_____
_____
_____

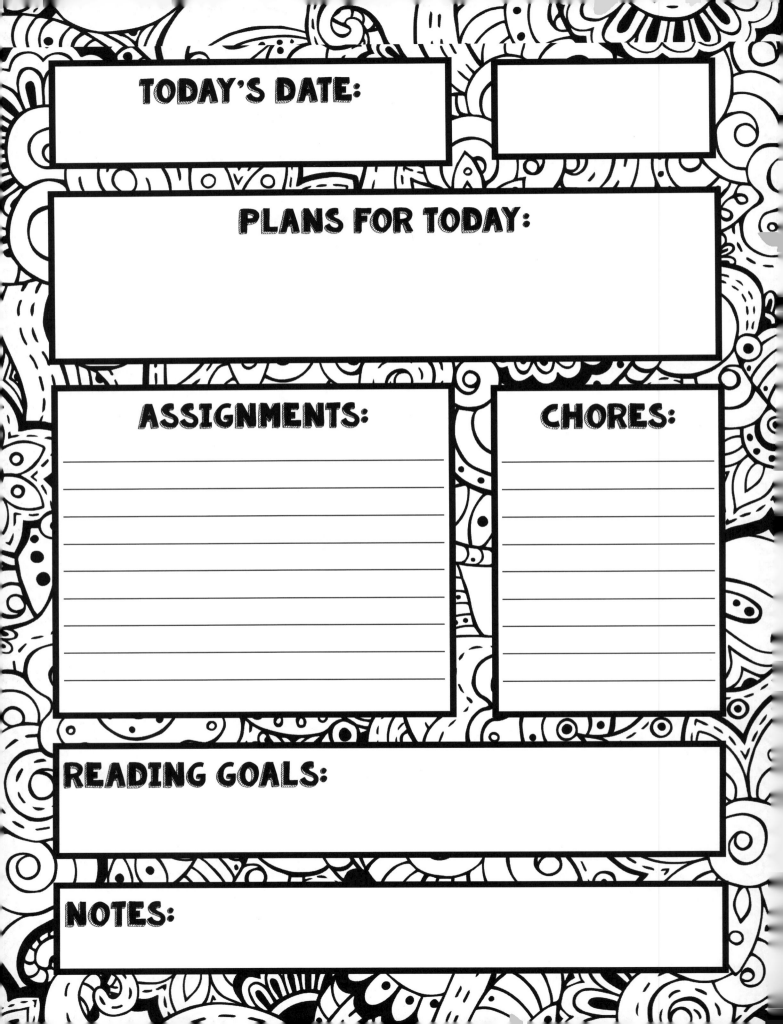

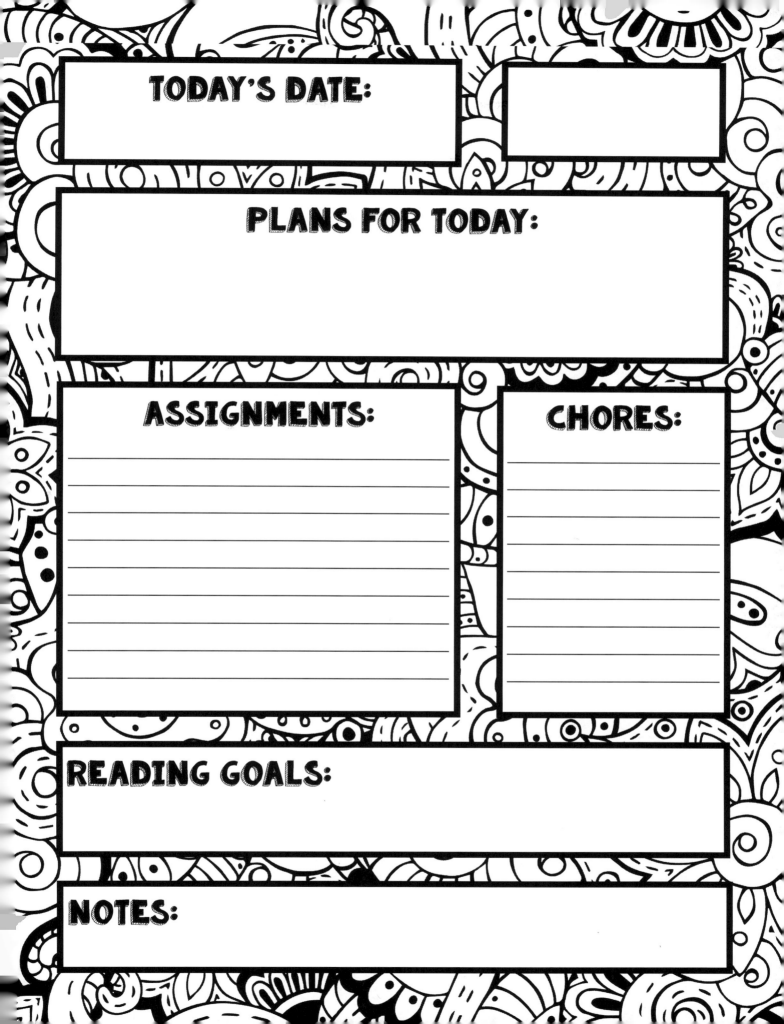

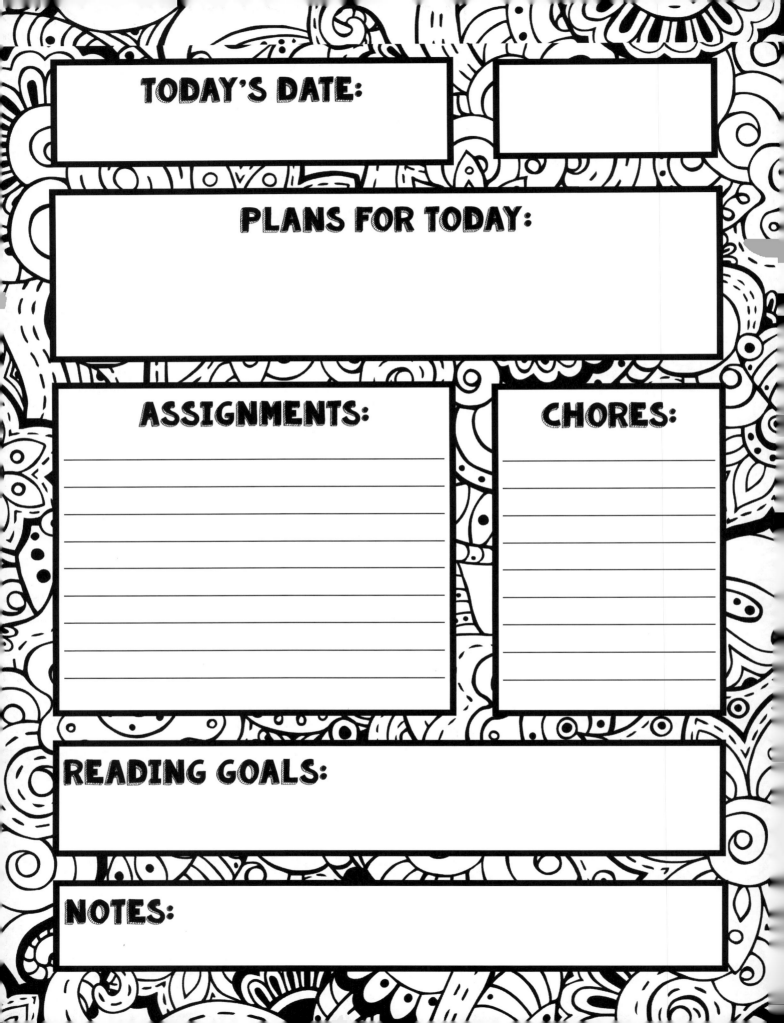

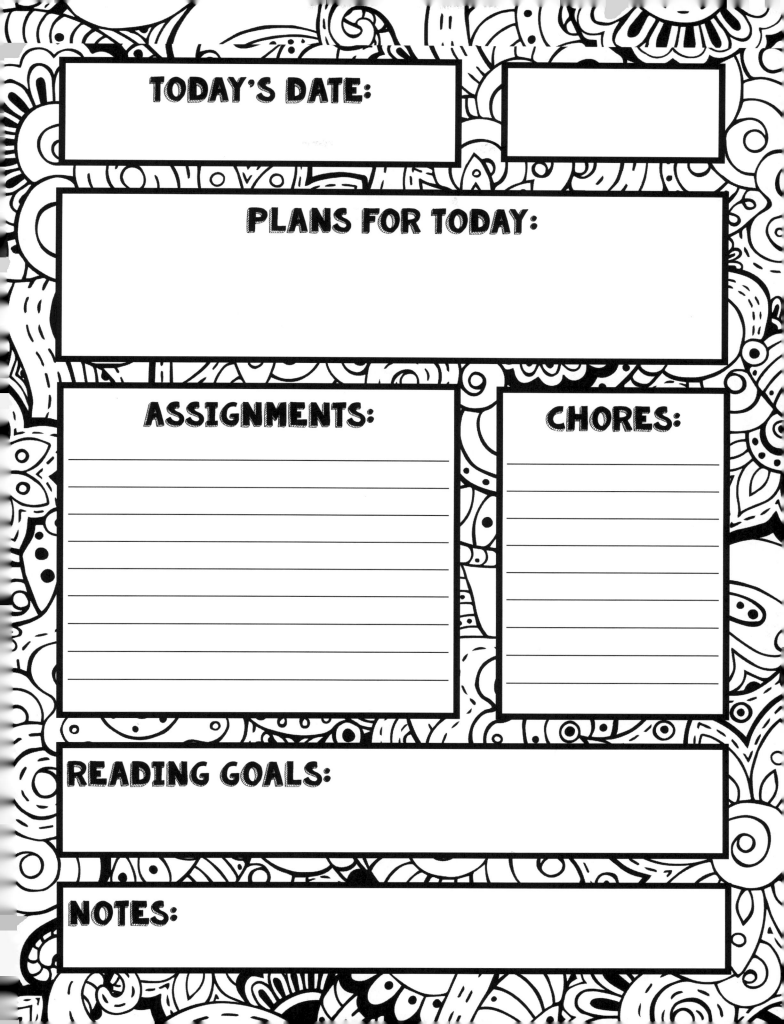

Plans & Perspective

"The home is the first and most effective place to learn the lessons of life: truth, honor, virtue, self control, the value of education, honest work, and the purpose and privilege of life." -McKay

My True Priorities

Long Term Goals

I Am Thankful For...

Checklist

Remember...

_____
_____
_____
_____
_____

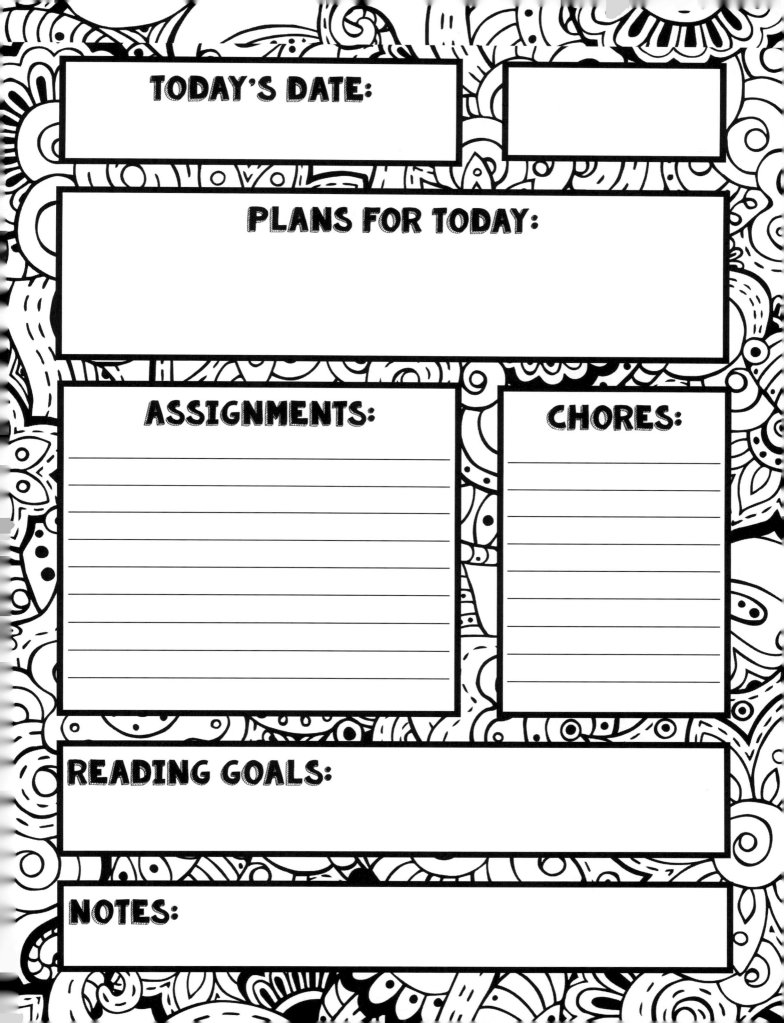

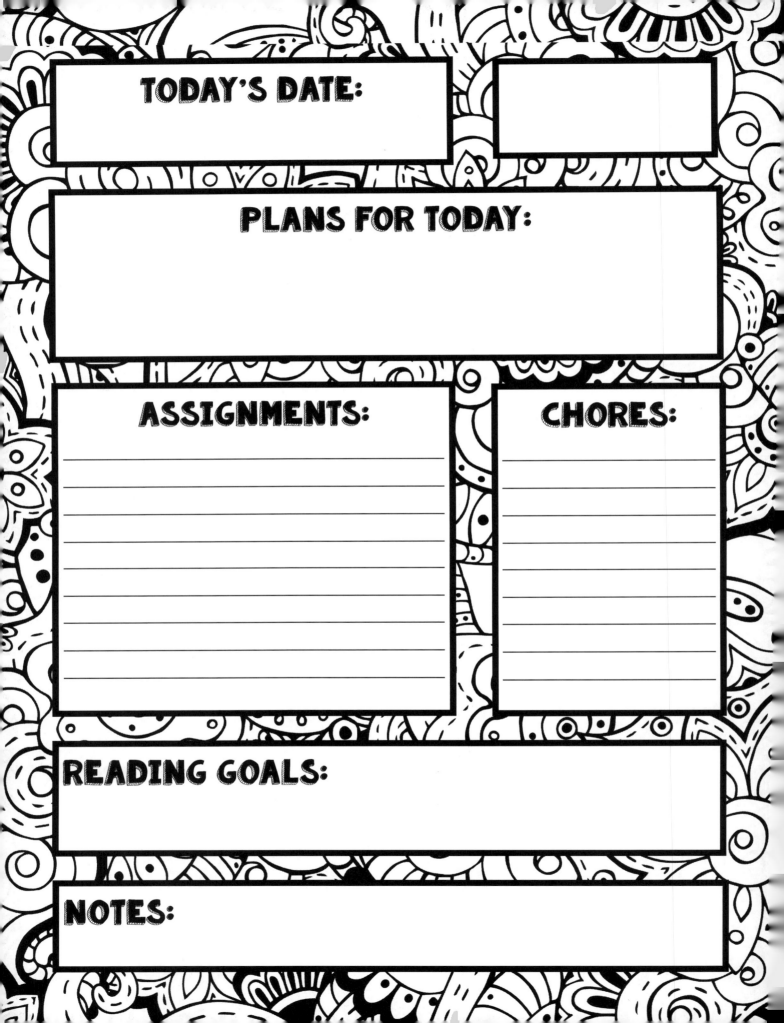

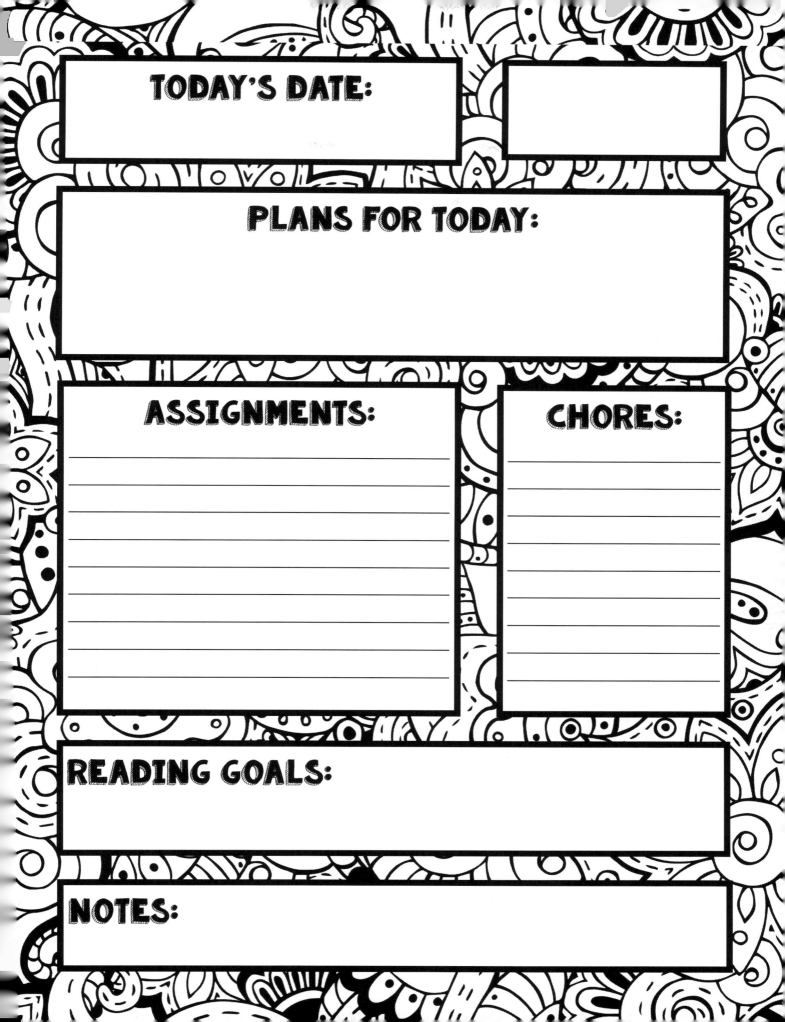

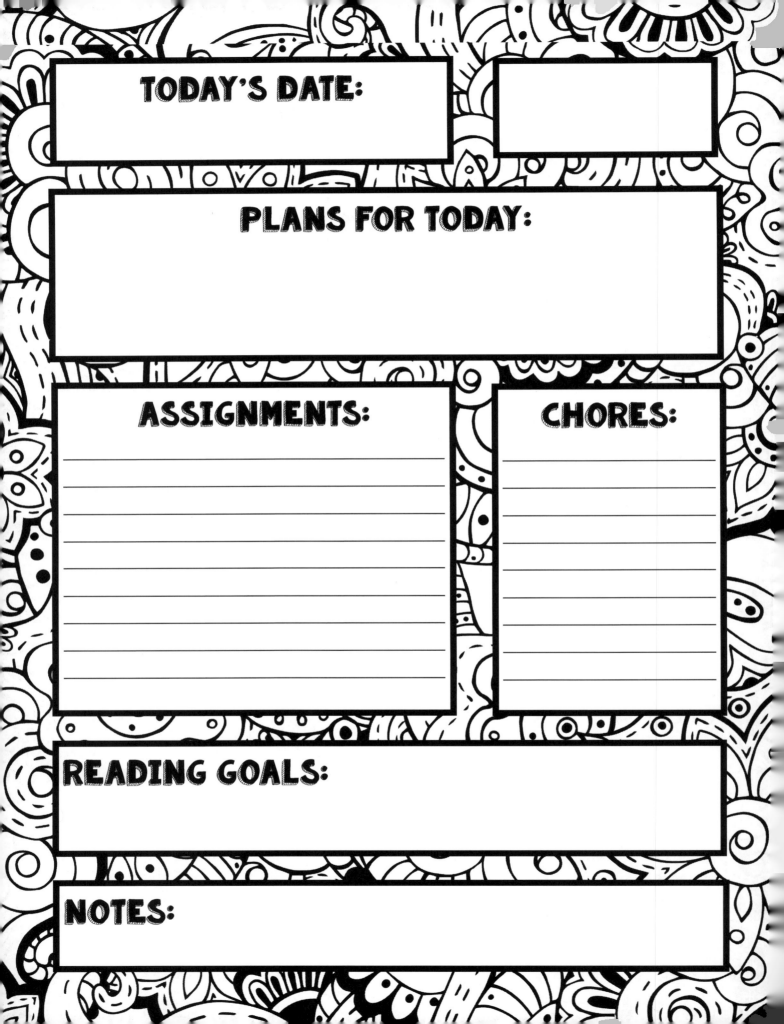

TODAY'S DATE:

PLANS FOR TODAY:

ASSIGNMENTS:

CHORES:

READING GOALS:

NOTES:

Plans & Perspective

"The home is the first and most effective place to learn the lessons of life: truth, honor, virtue, self control, the value of education, honest work, and the purpose and privilege of life." -McKay

My True Priorities

Long Term Goals

I Am Thankful For...

Checklist

Remember...

_____
_____
_____
_____
_____

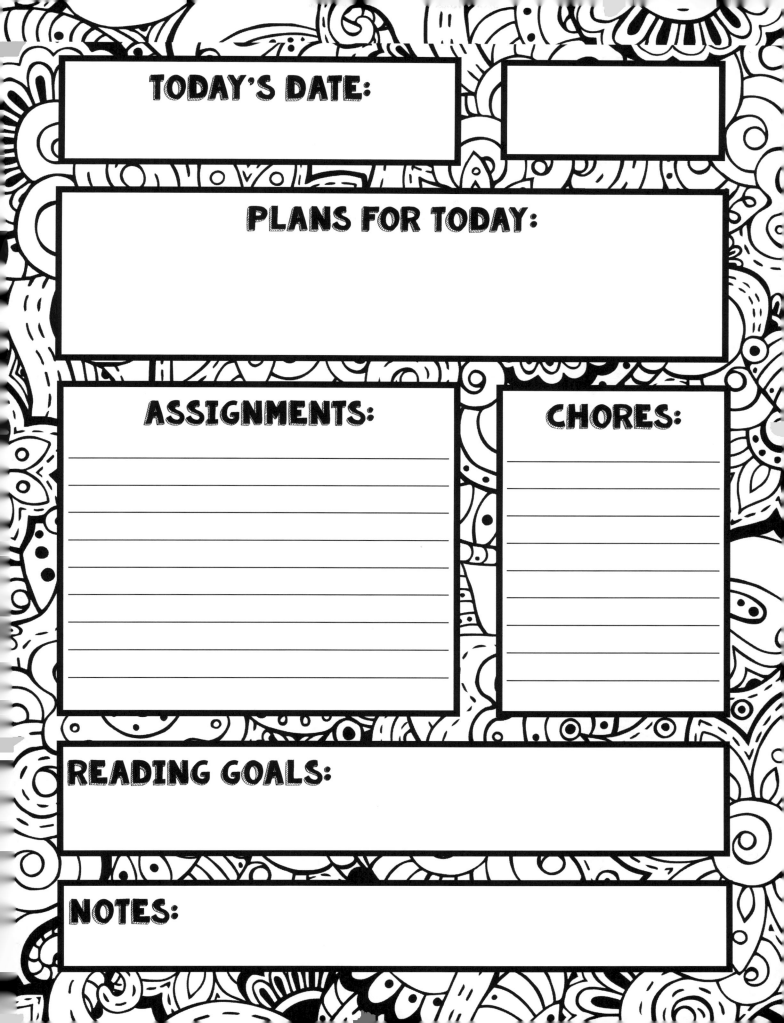

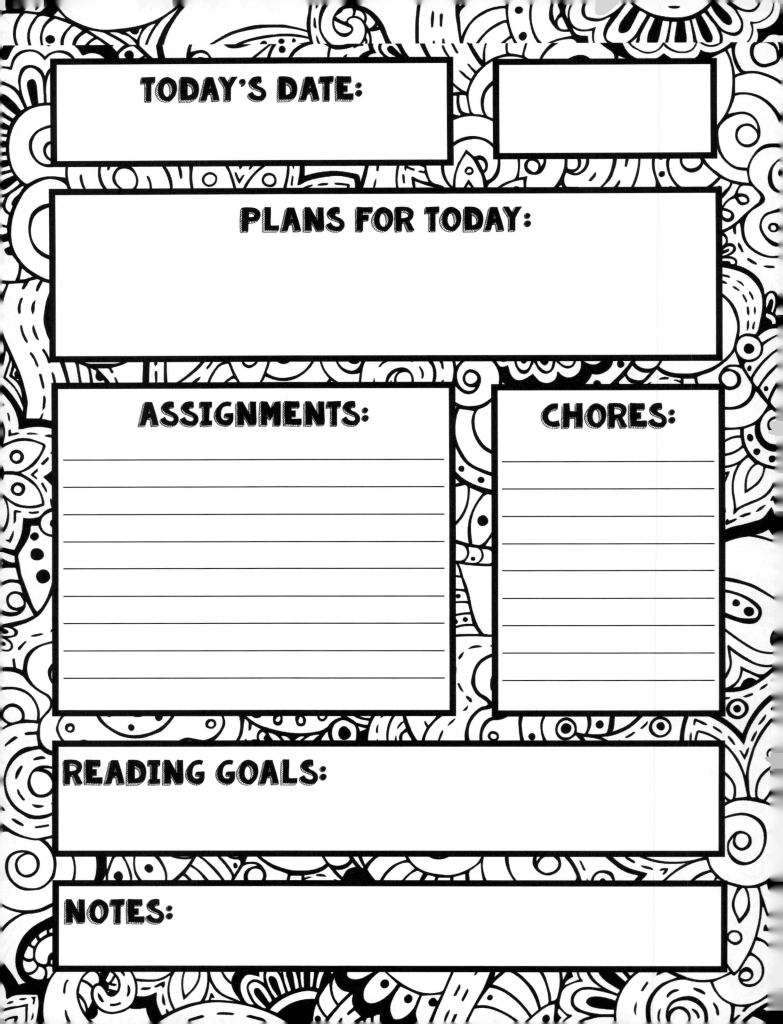

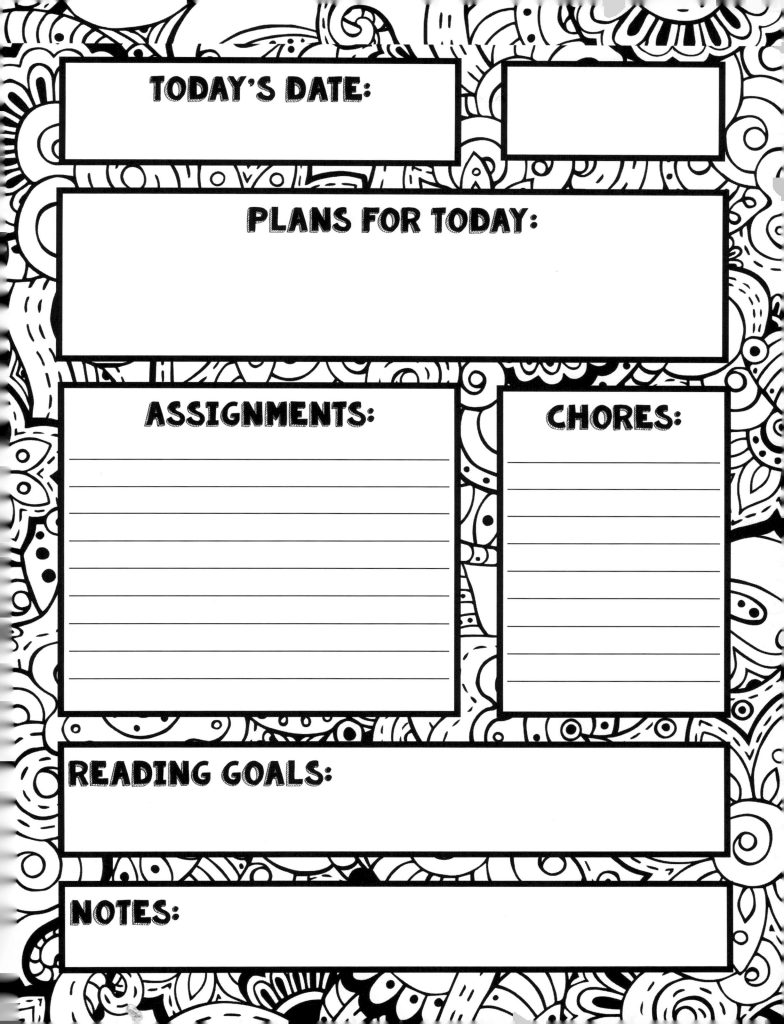

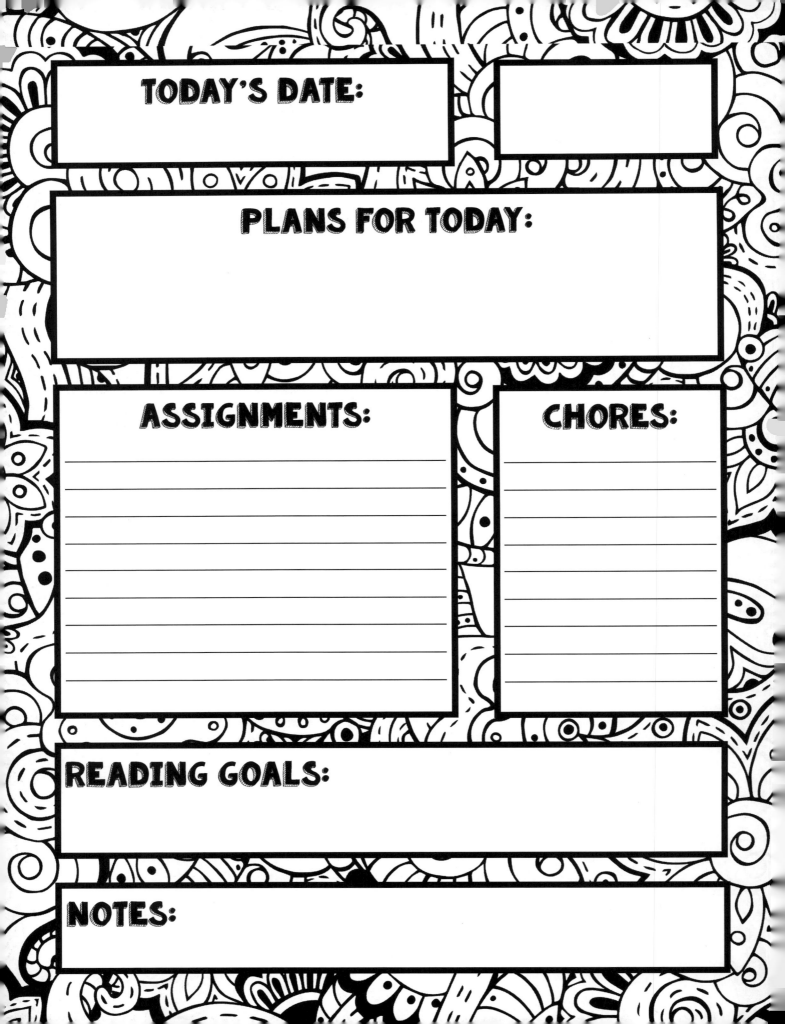

Plans & Perspective

"The home is the first and most effective place to learn the lessons of life: truth, honor, virtue, self control, the value of education, honest work, and the purpose and privilege of life." -McKay

My True Priorities

Long Term Goals

I Am Thankful For...

Checklist

Remember...

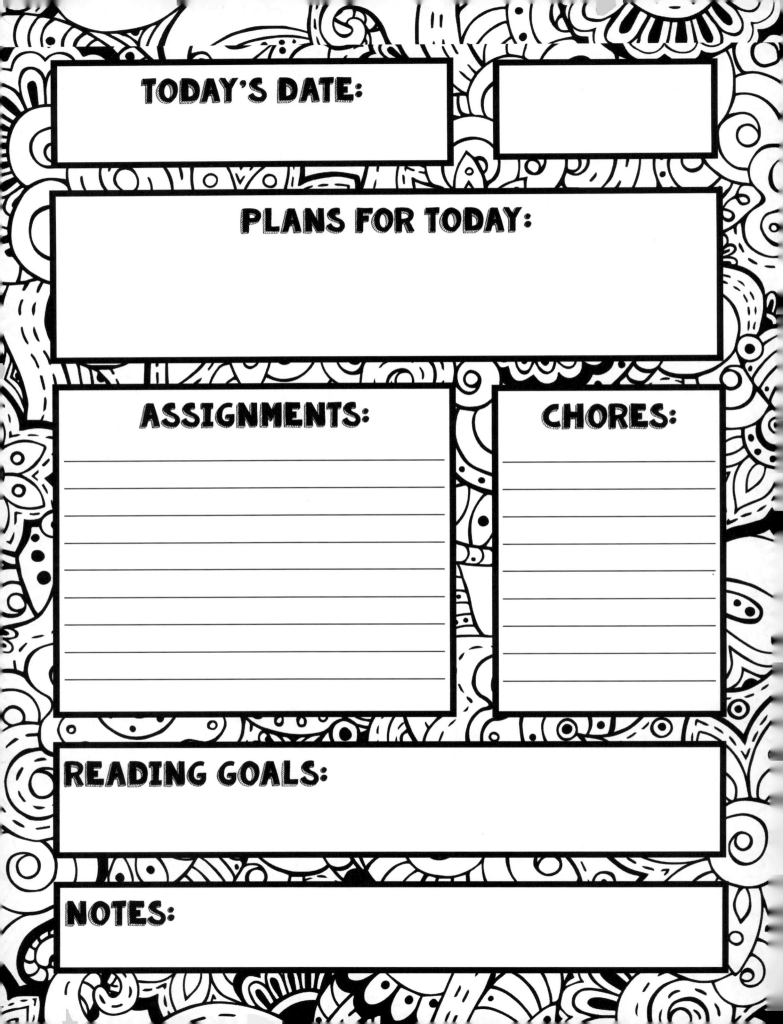

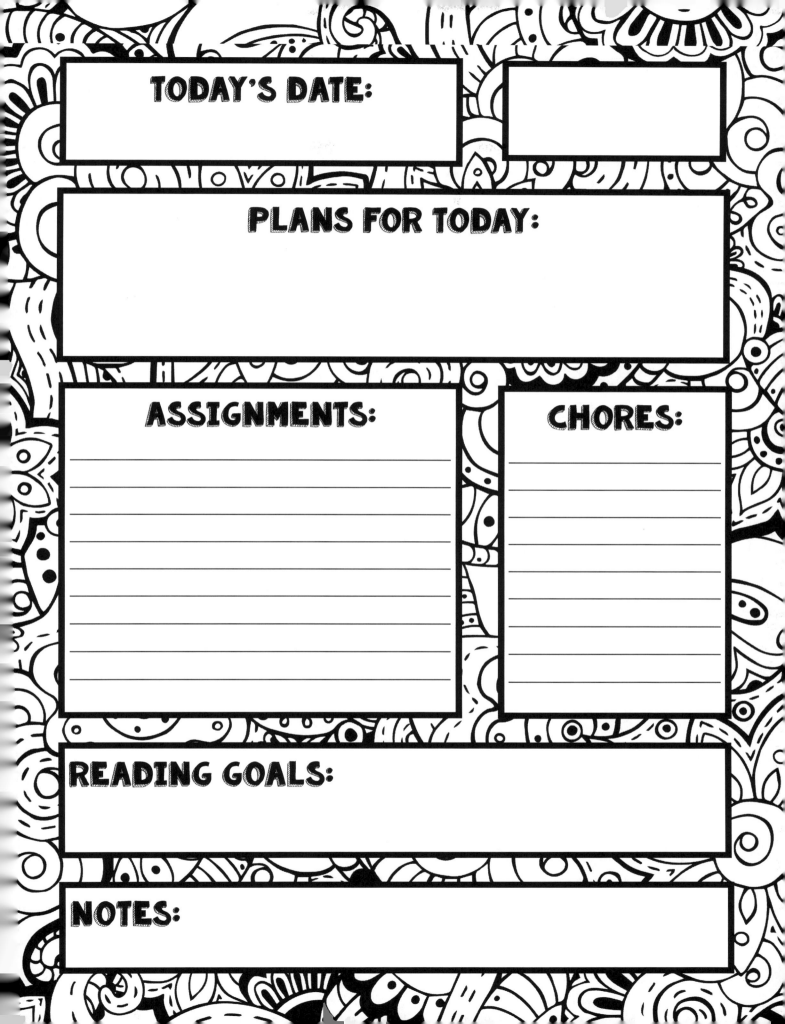

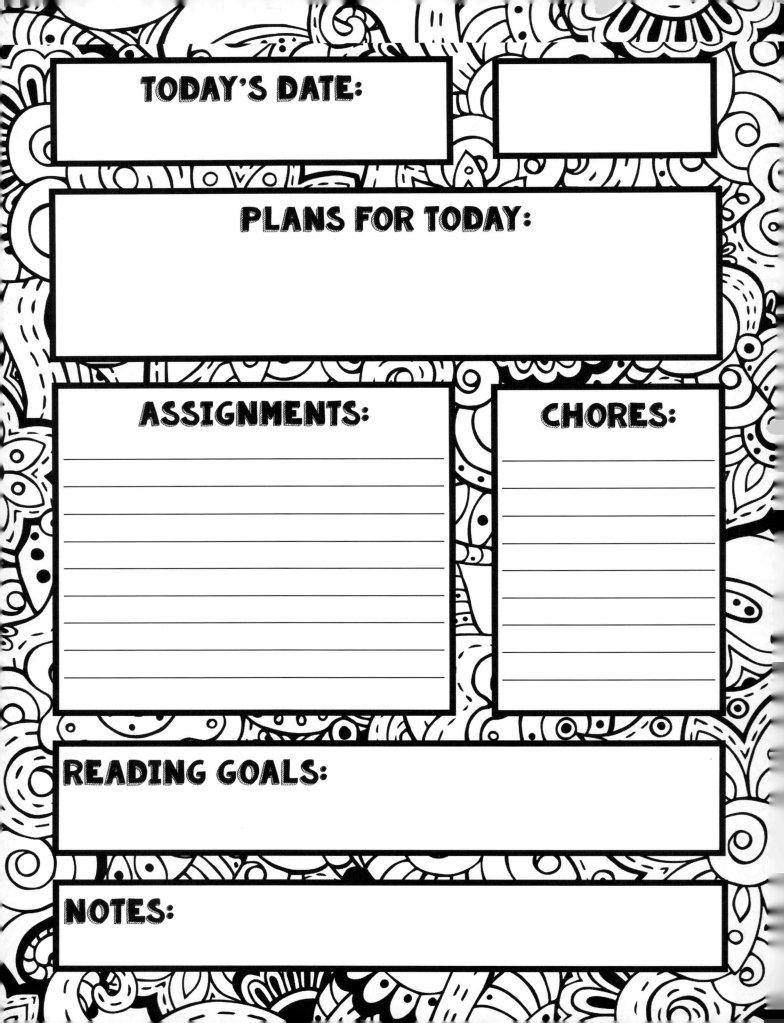

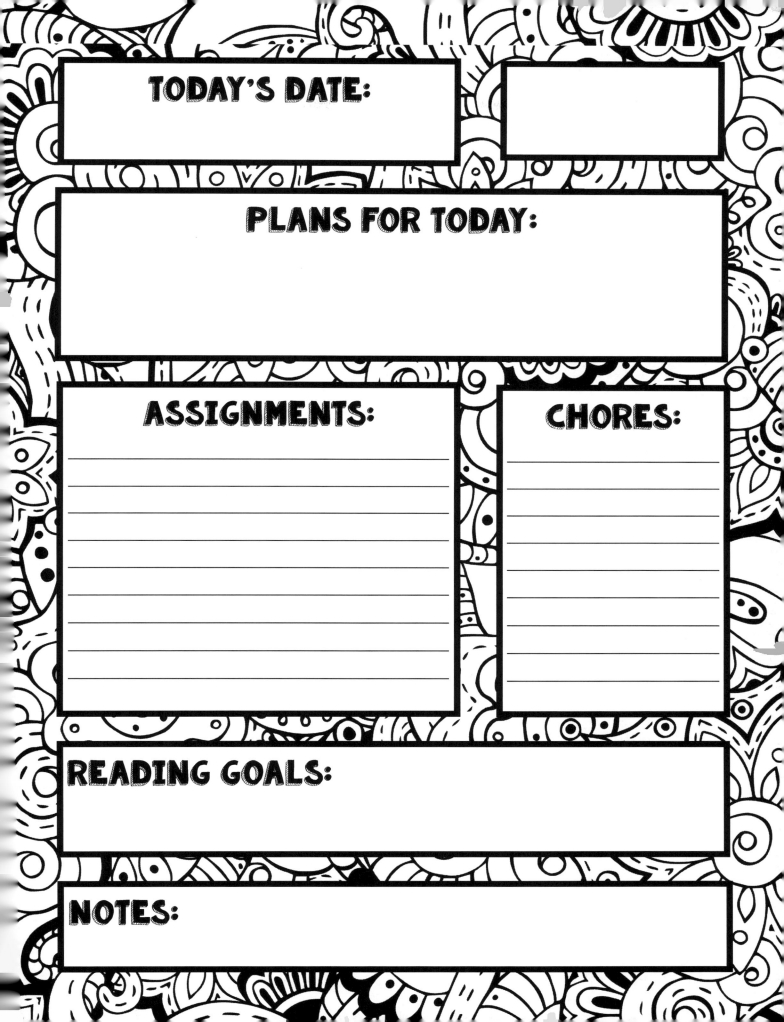

Plans & Perspective

"The home is the first and most effective place to learn the lessons of life: truth, honor, virtue, self control, the value of education, honest work, and the purpose and privilege of life." -McKay

My True Priorities

Long Term Goals

I Am Thankful For...

Checklist

Remember...

_____
_____
_____
_____
_____

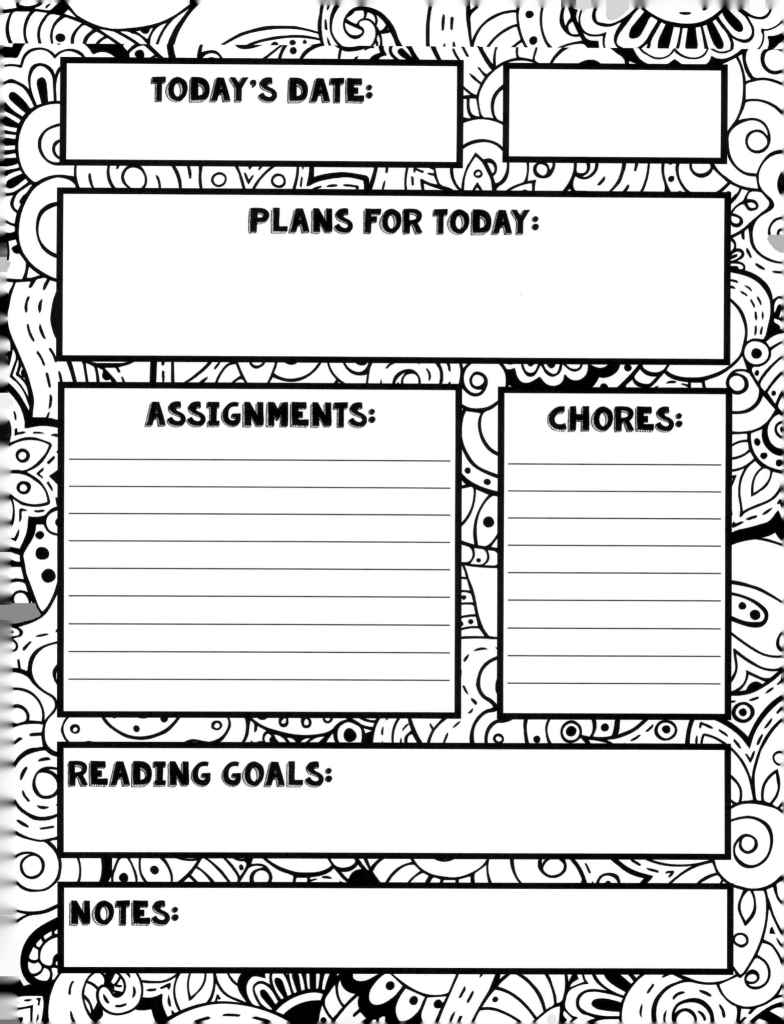

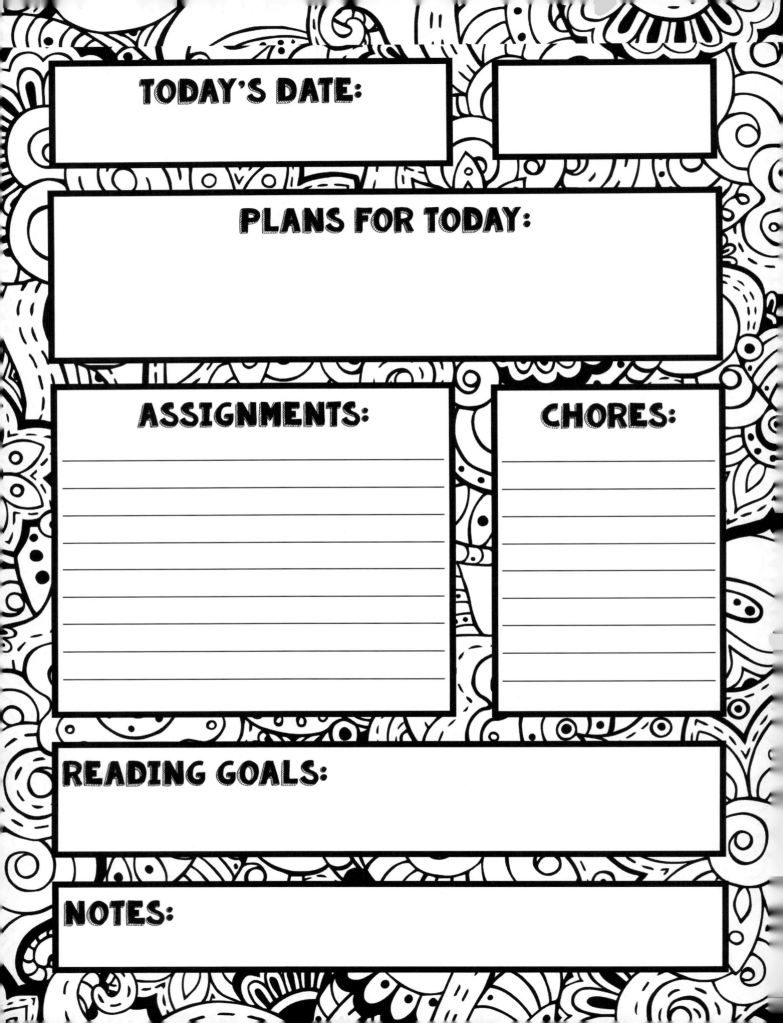

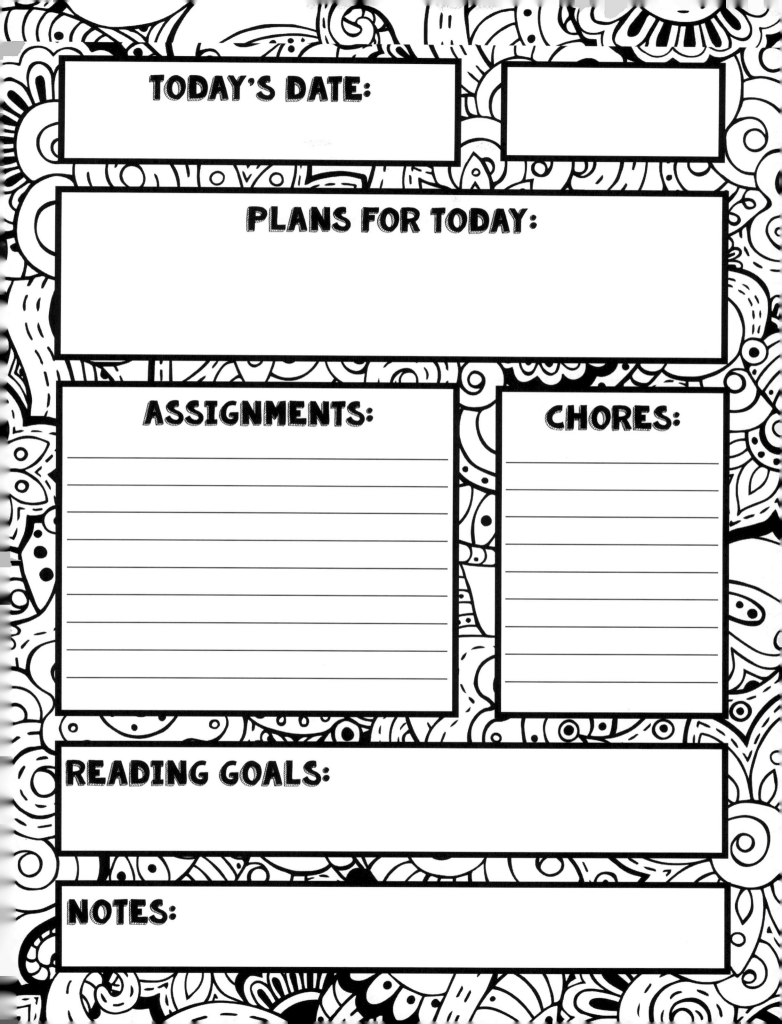

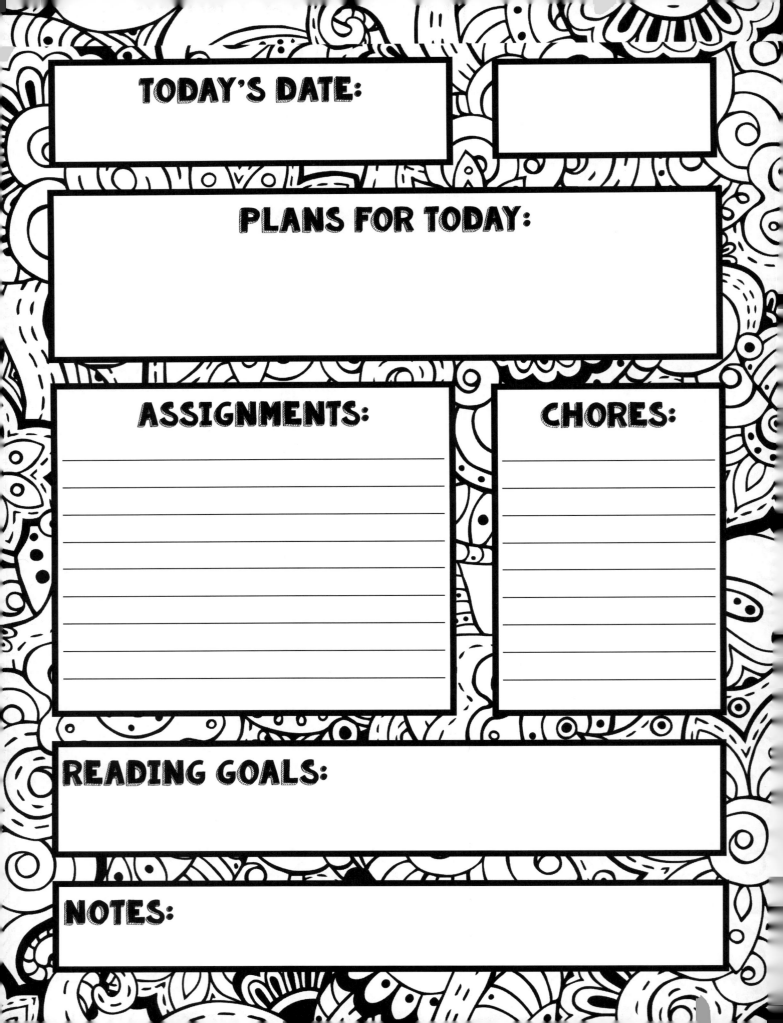

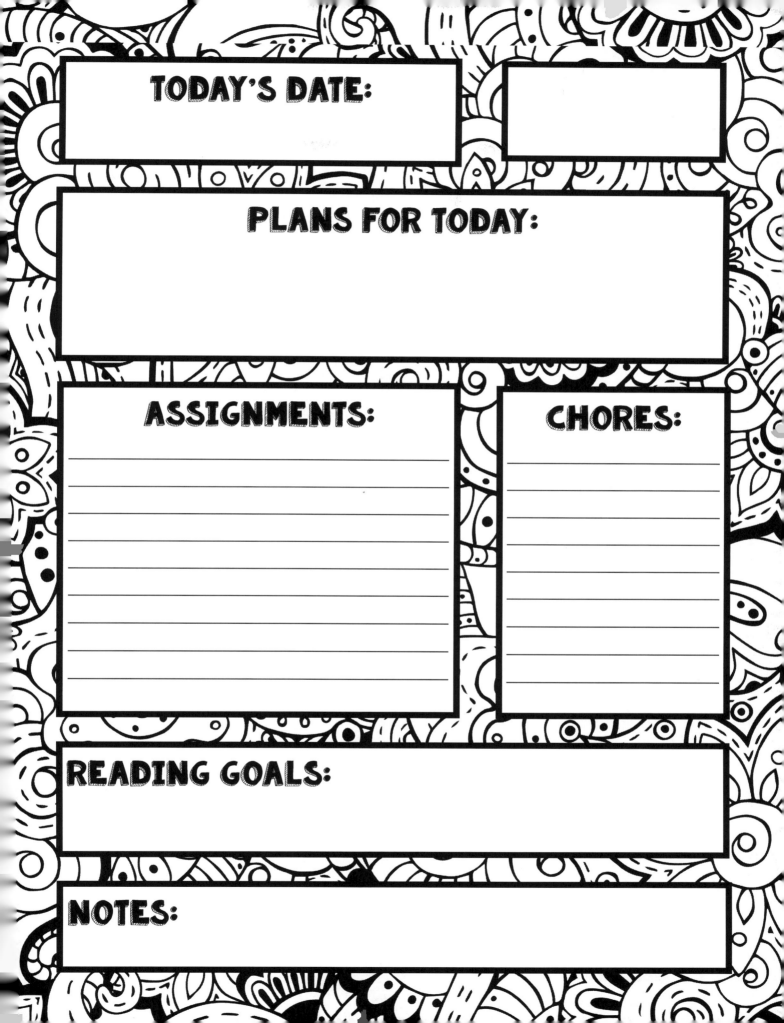

Plans & Perspective

"The home is the first and most effective place to learn the lessons of life: truth, honor, virtue, self control, the value of education, honest work, and the purpose and privilege of life." -McKay

My True Priorities

Long Term Goals

I Am Thankful For...

Checklist

Remember...

_____
_____
_____
_____
_____

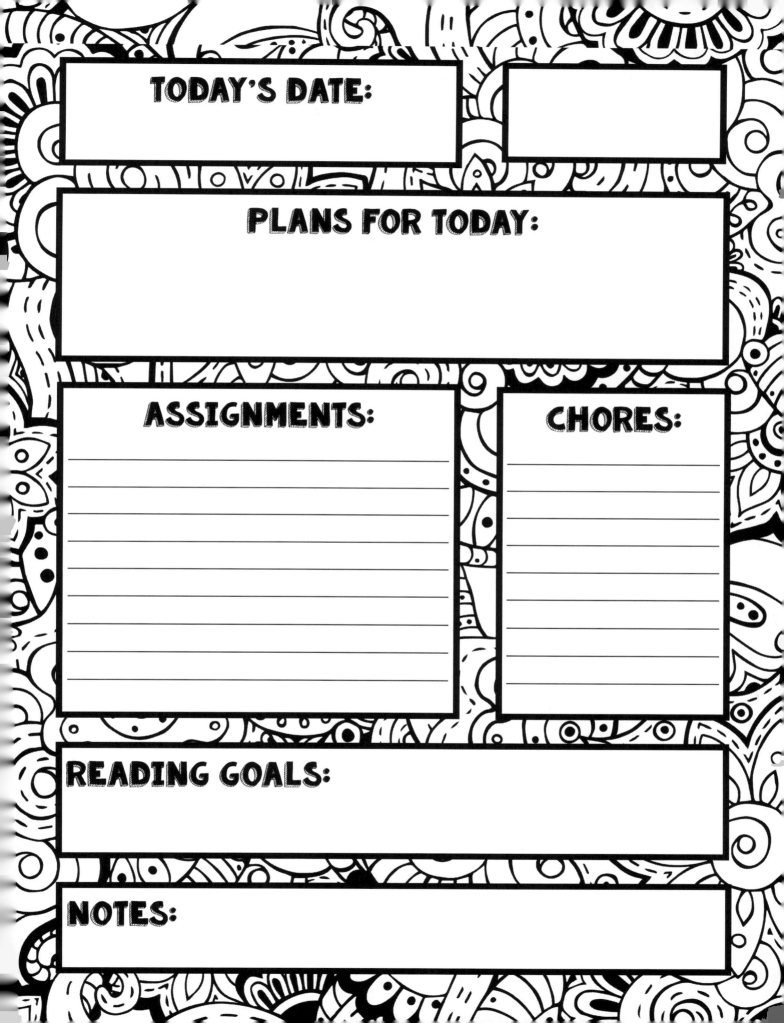

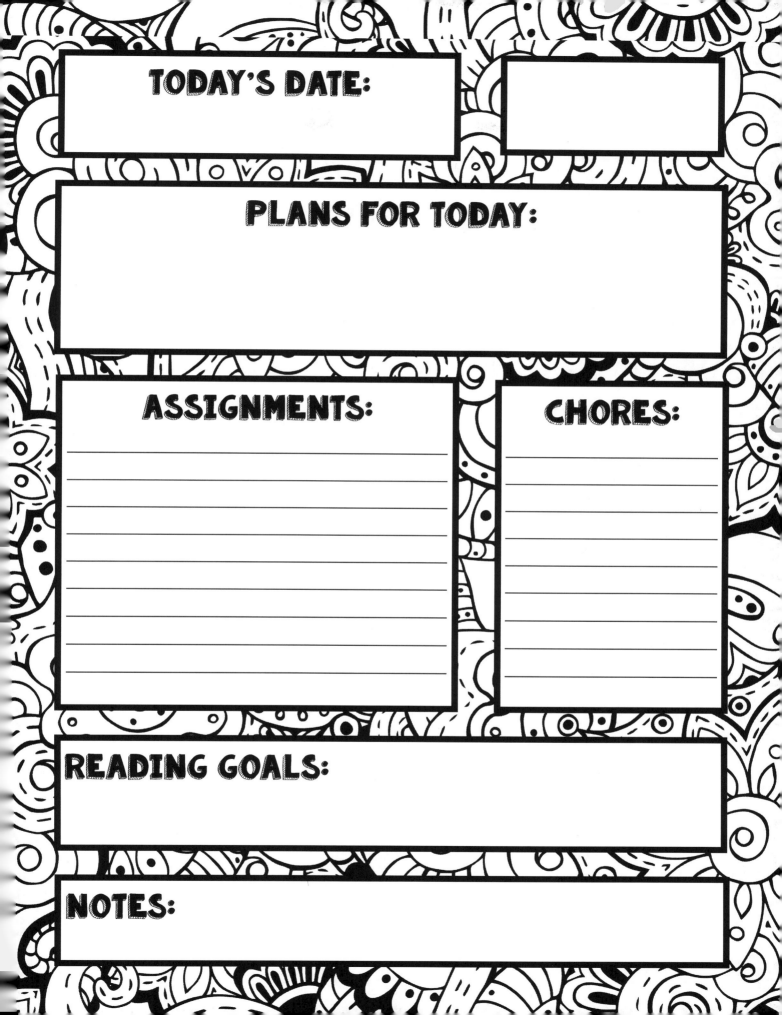

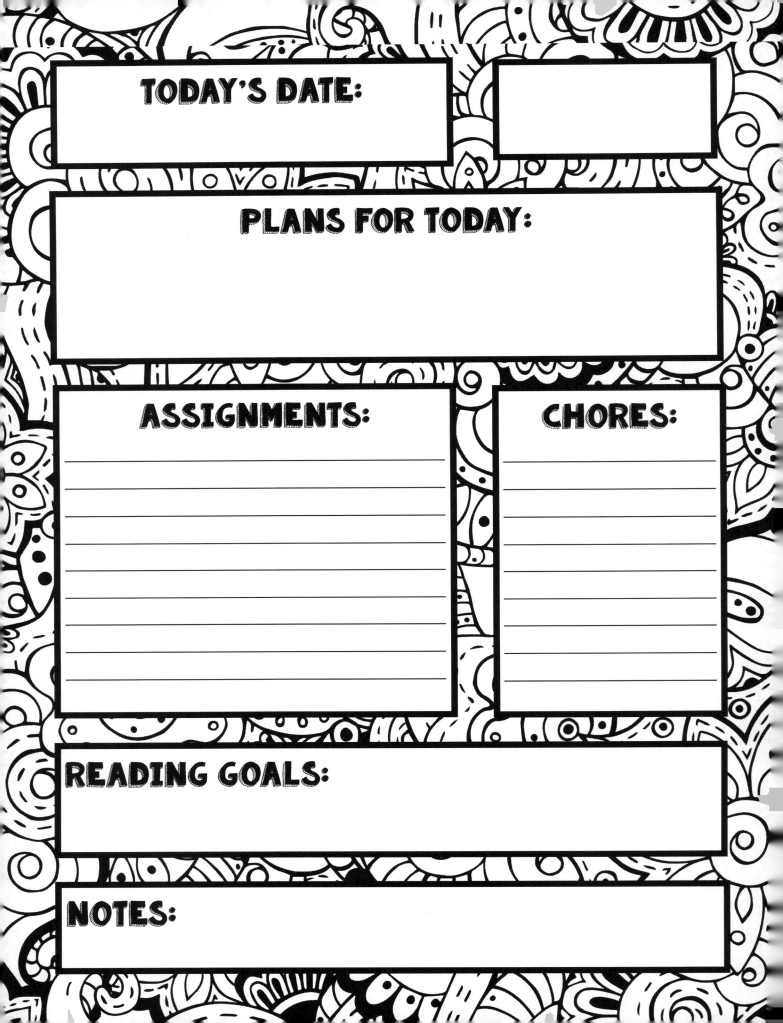

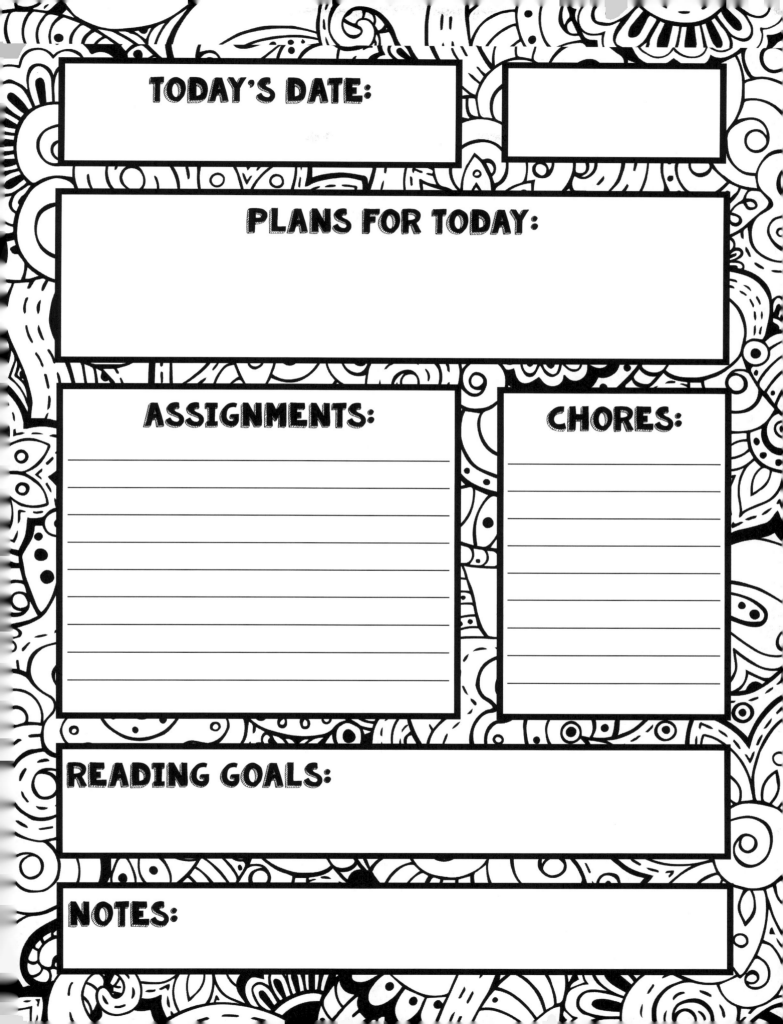

Plans & Perspective

"The home is the first and most effective place to learn the lessons of life: truth, honor, virtue, self control, the value of education, honest work, and the purpose and privilege of life." -McKay

My True Priorities

Long Term Goals

I Am Thankful For...

Checklist

Remember...

_____
_____
_____
_____
_____

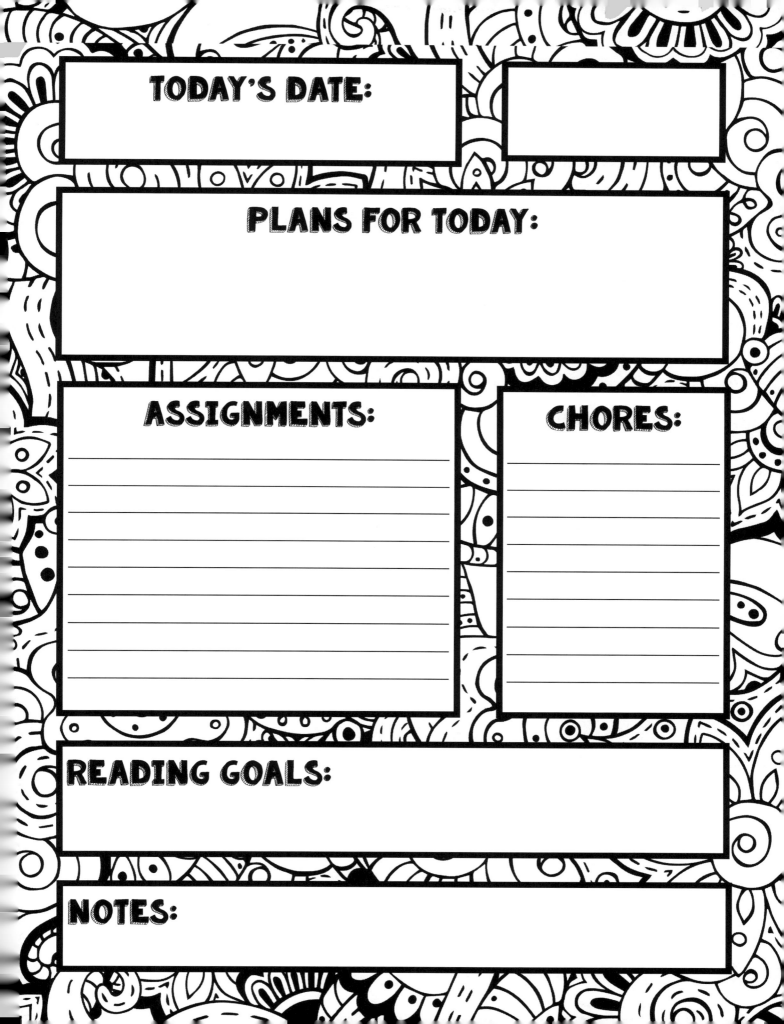

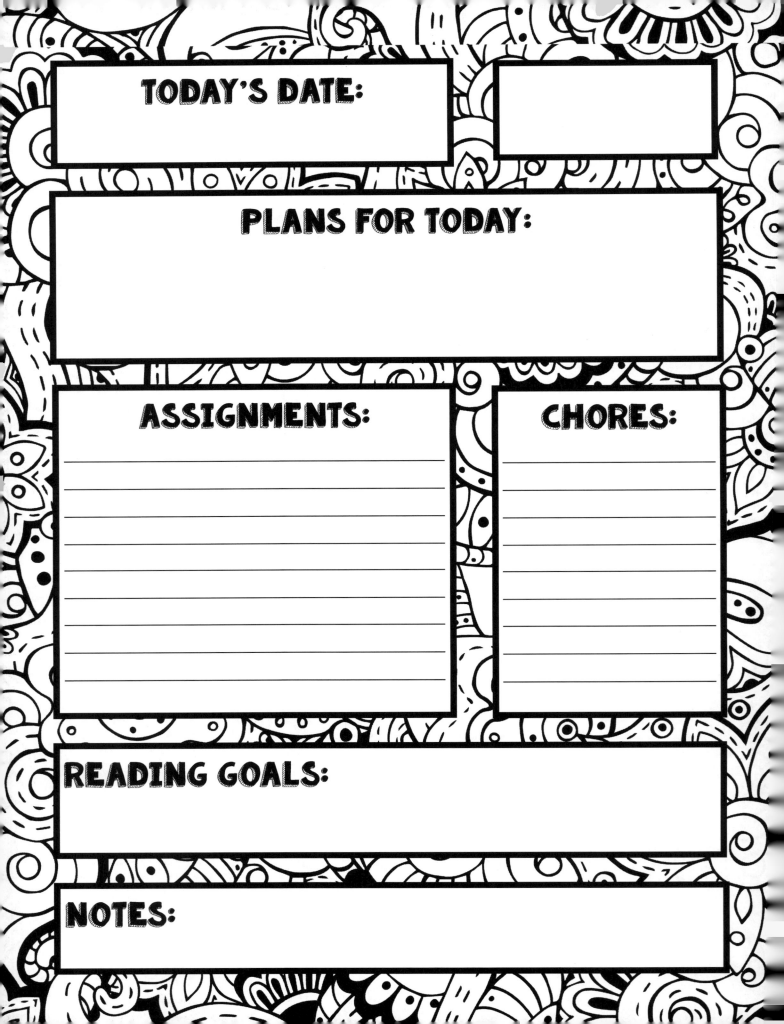

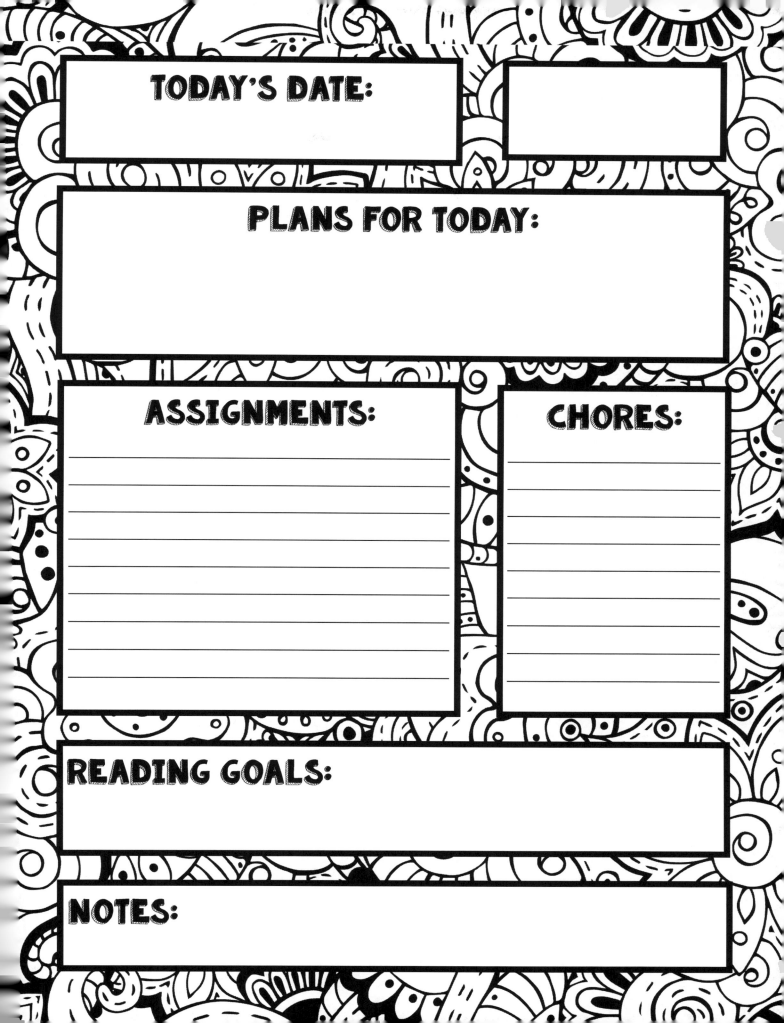

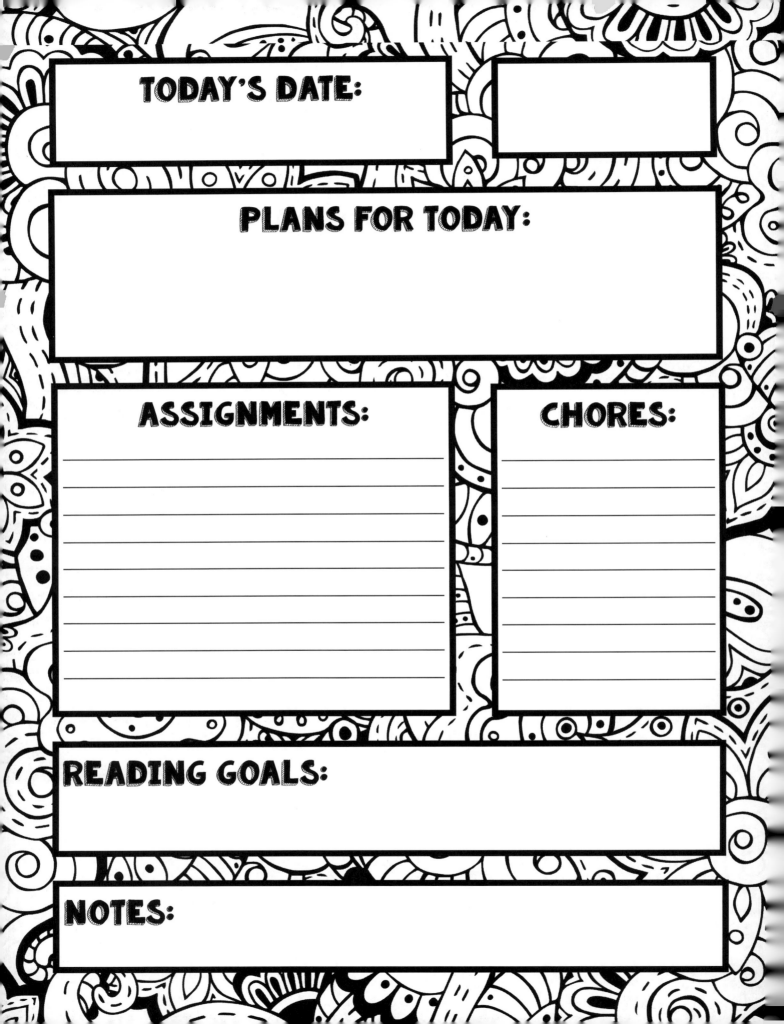

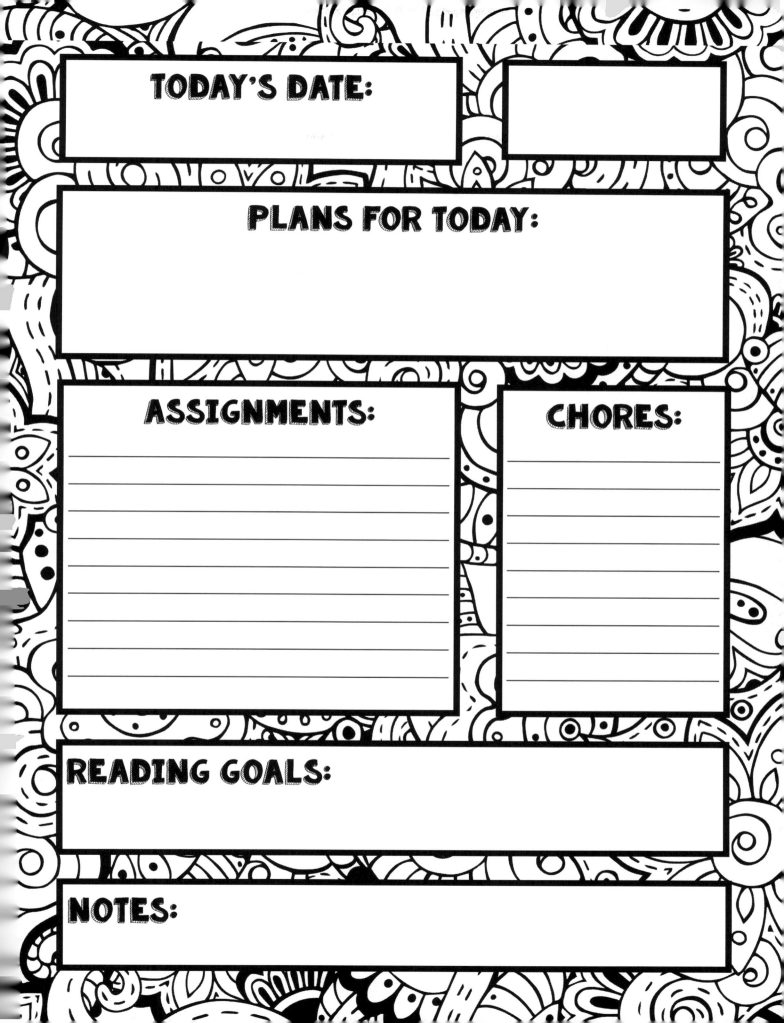

Plans & Perspective

"The home is the first and most effective place to learn the lessons of life: truth, honor, virtue, self control, the value of education, honest work, and the purpose and privilege of life." -McKay

My True Priorities

Long Term Goals

I Am Thankful For...

Checklist

Remember...

_____
_____
_____
_____
_____

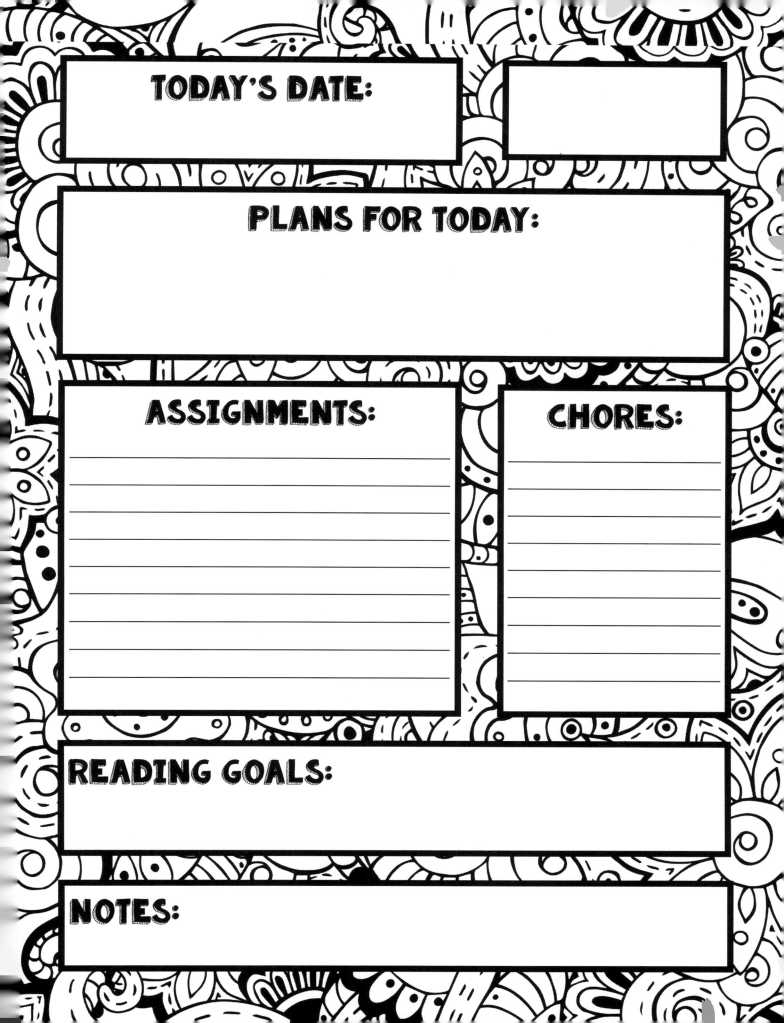

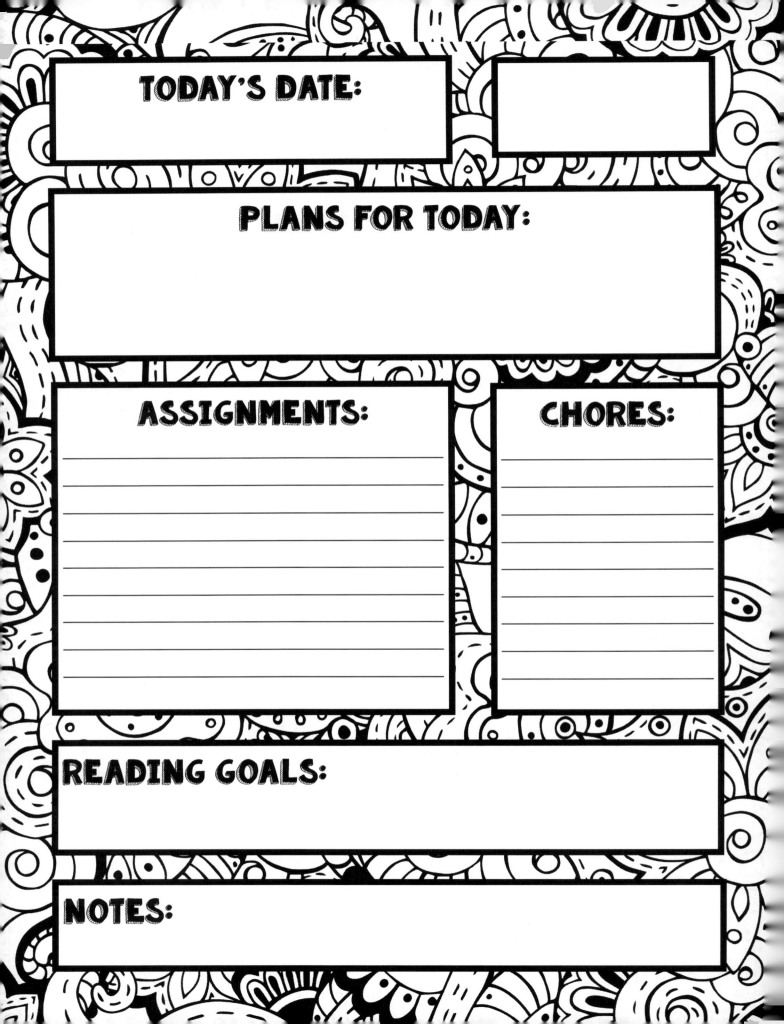

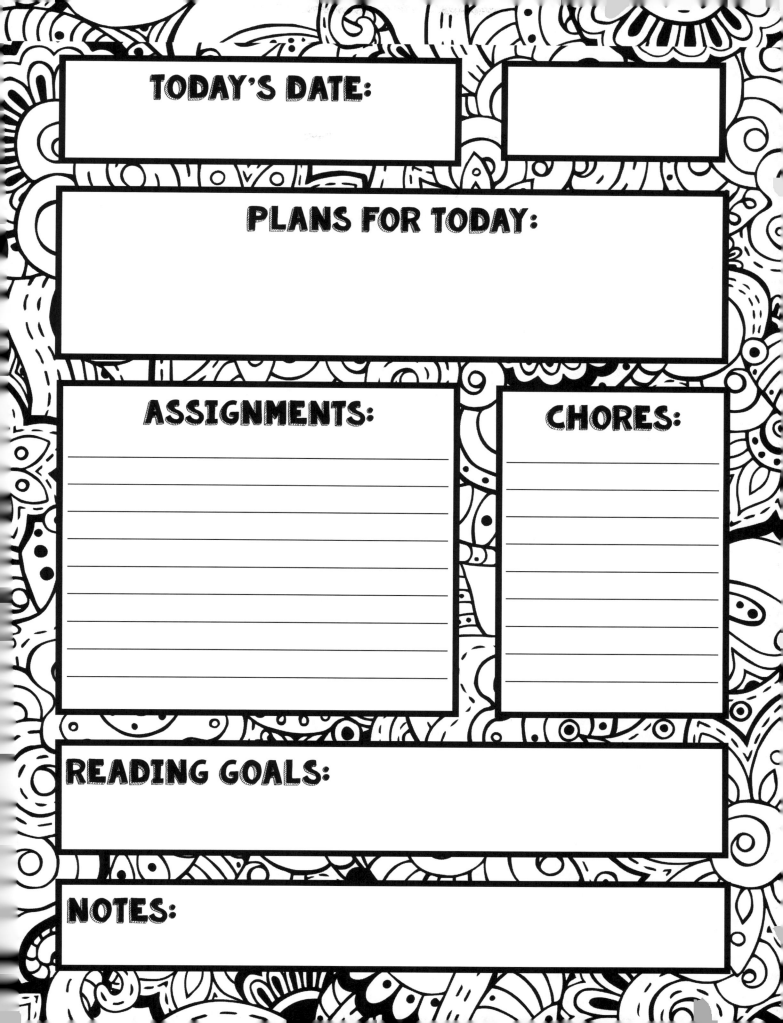

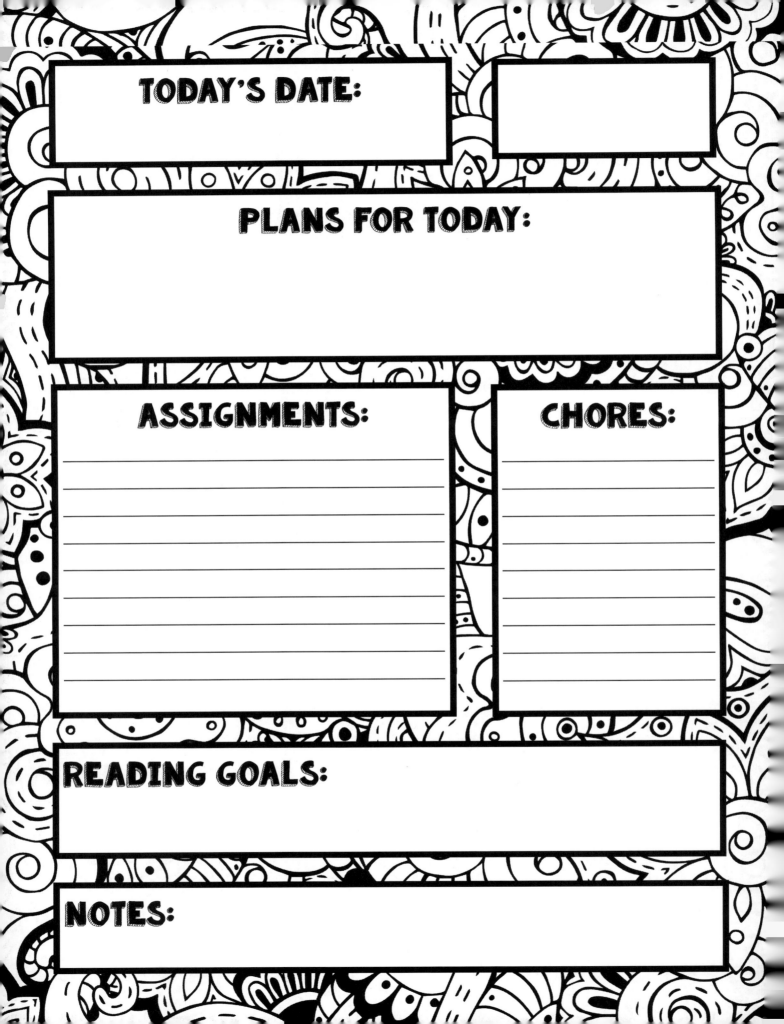

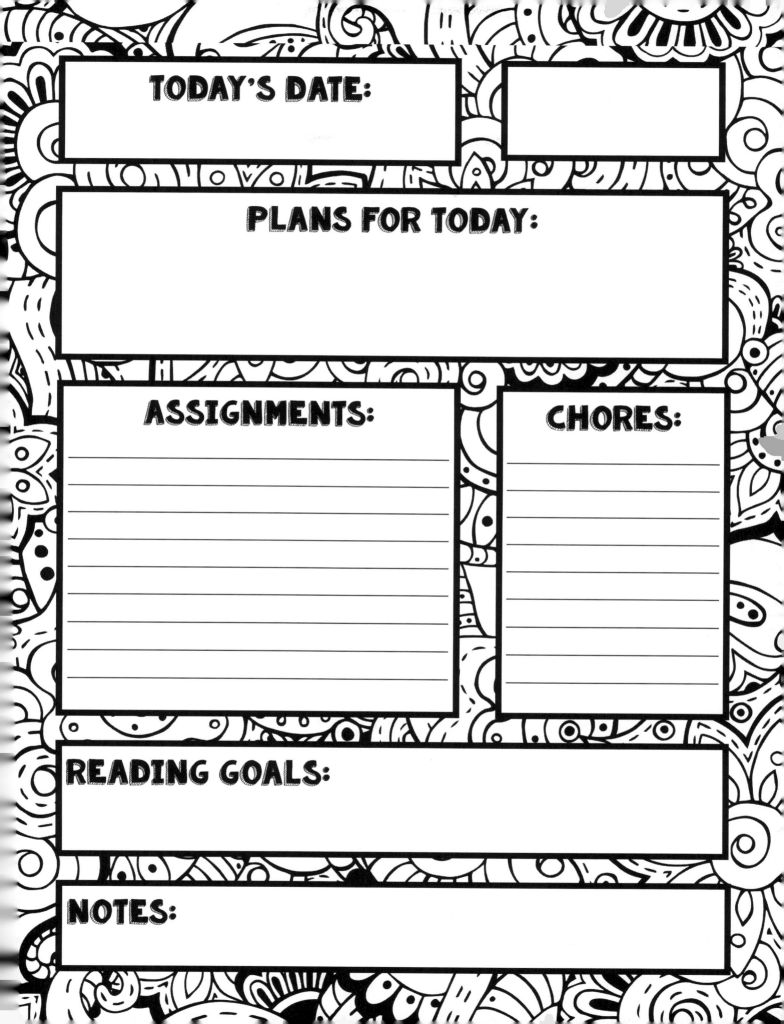

Plans & Perspective

"The home is the first and most effective place to learn the lessons of life: truth, honor, virtue, self control, the value of education, honest work, and the purpose and privilege of life." -McKay

My True Priorities

Long Term Goals

I Am Thankful For...

Checklist

Remember...

_____
_____
_____
_____
_____

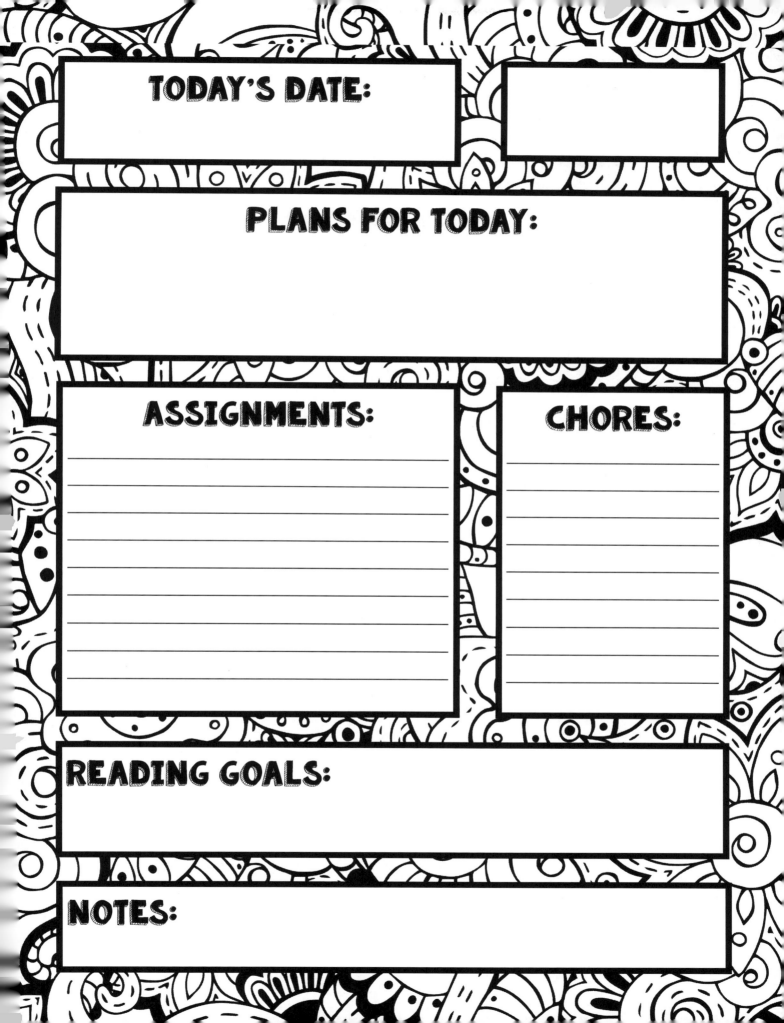

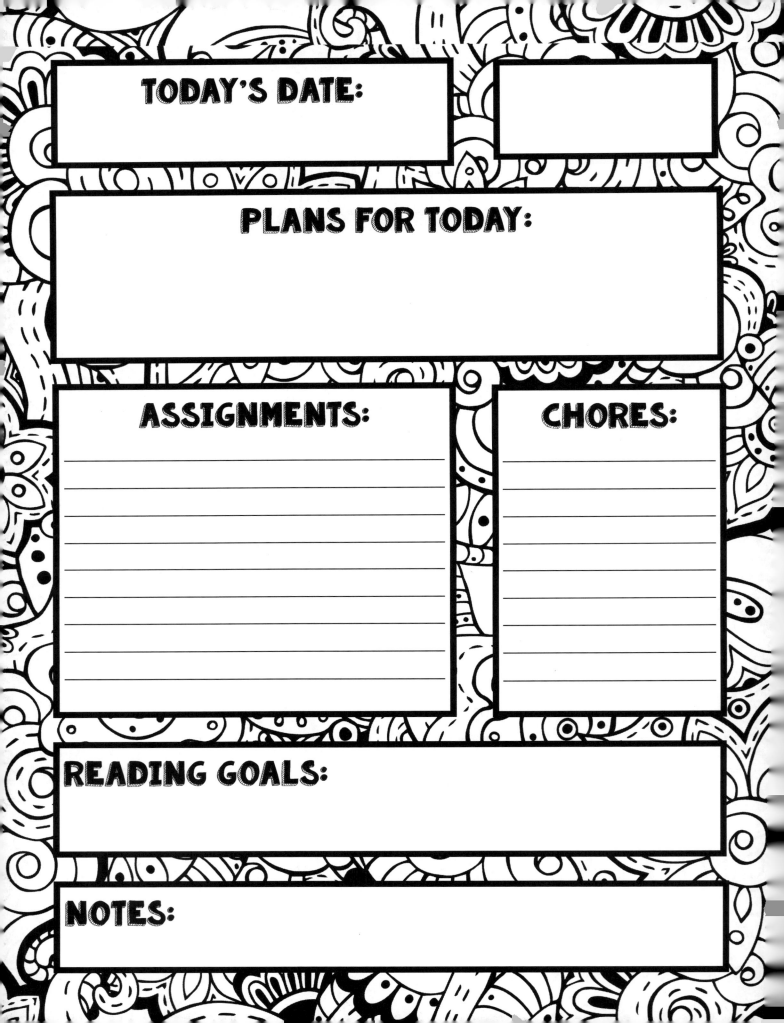

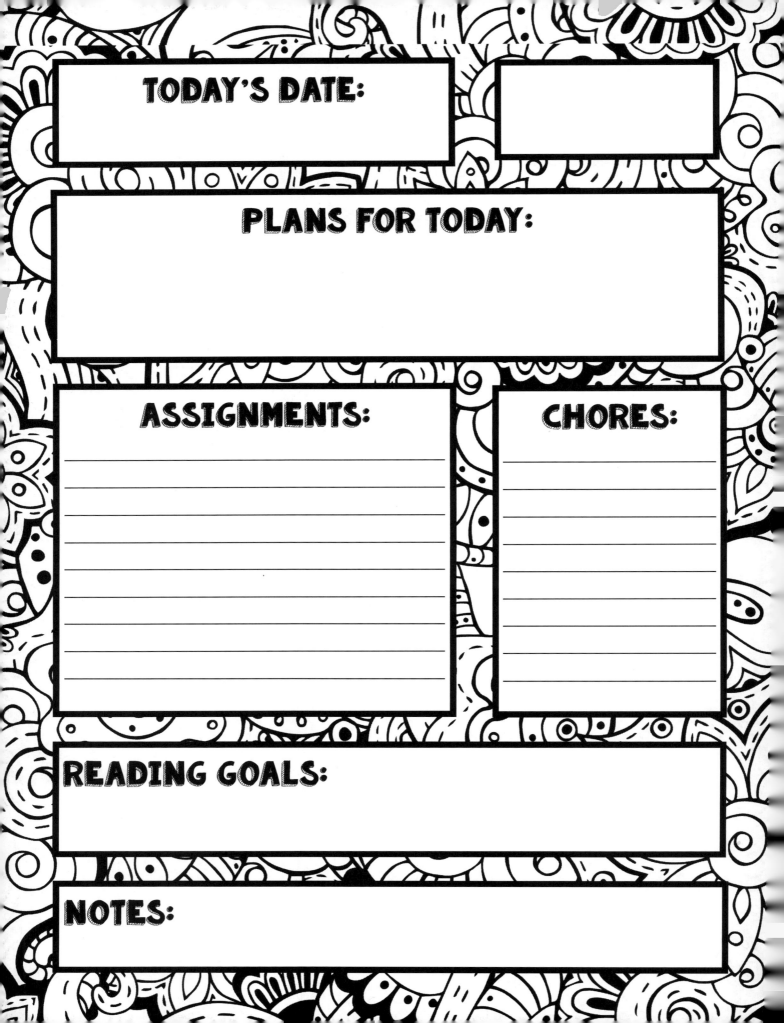

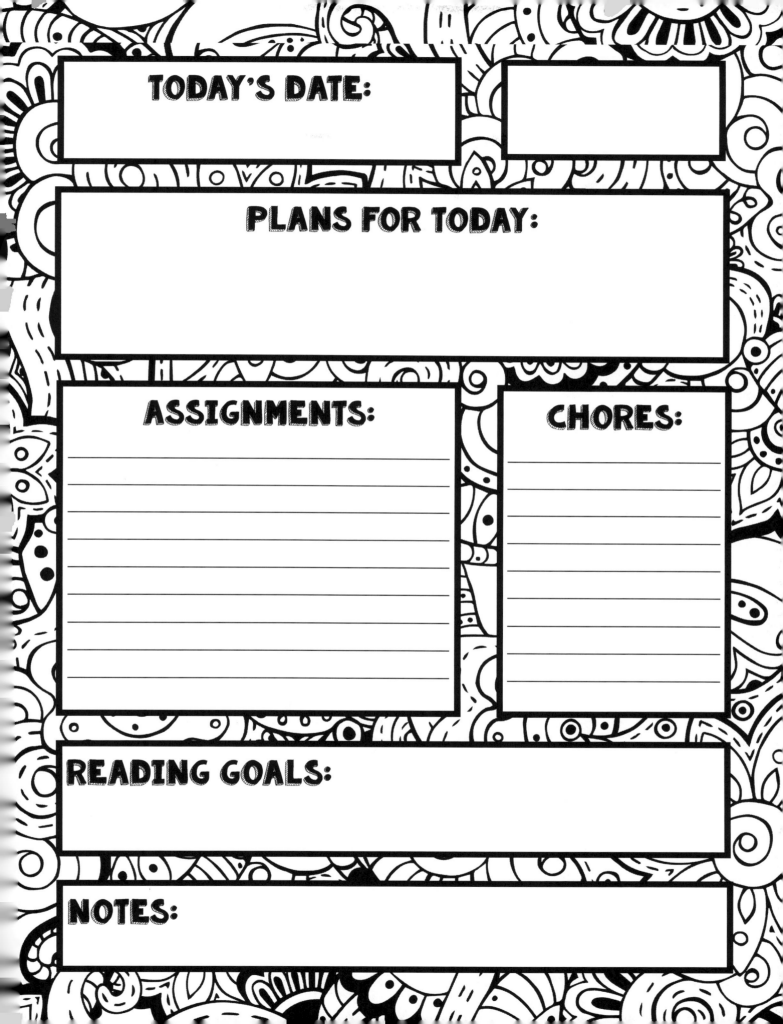

Plans & Perspective

"The home is the first and most effective place to learn the lessons of life: truth, honor, virtue, self control, the value of education, honest work, and the purpose and privilege of life." -McKay

My True Priorities

Long Term Goals

I Am Thankful For...

Checklist

_____
_____
_____
_____
_____

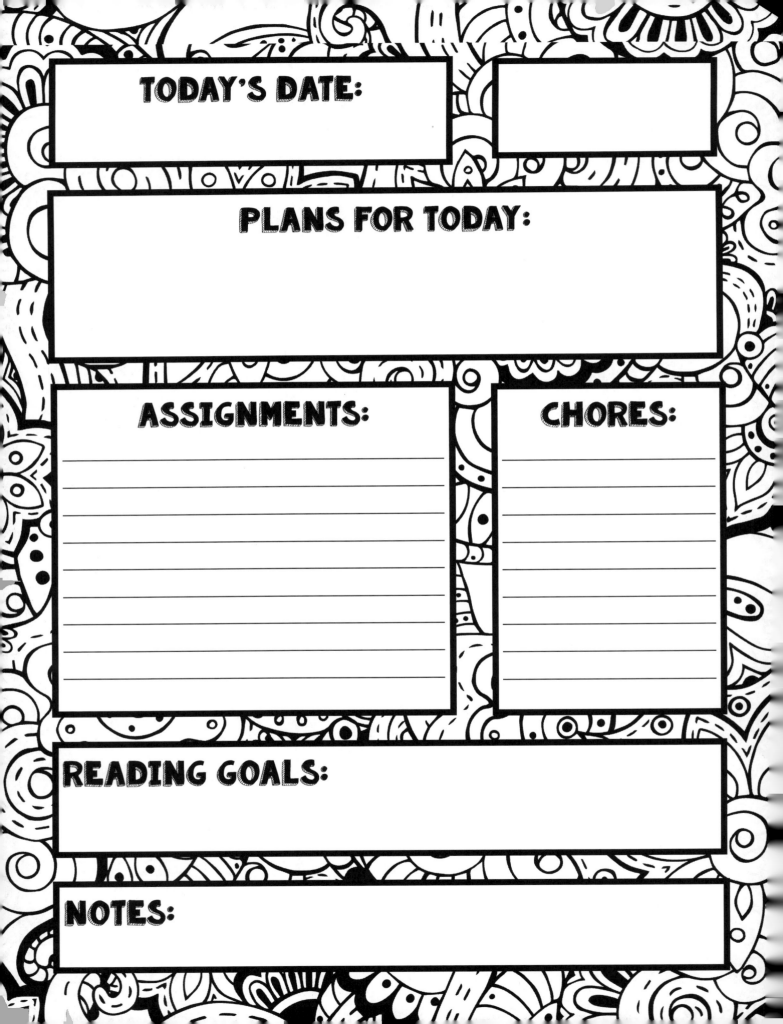

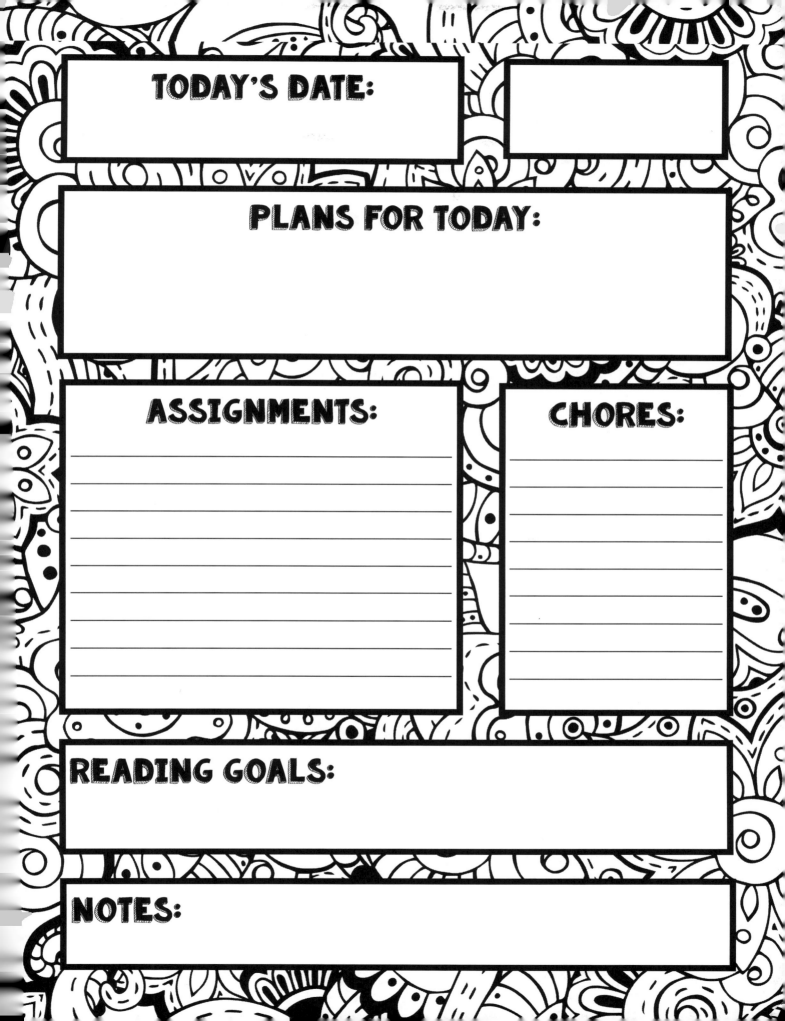

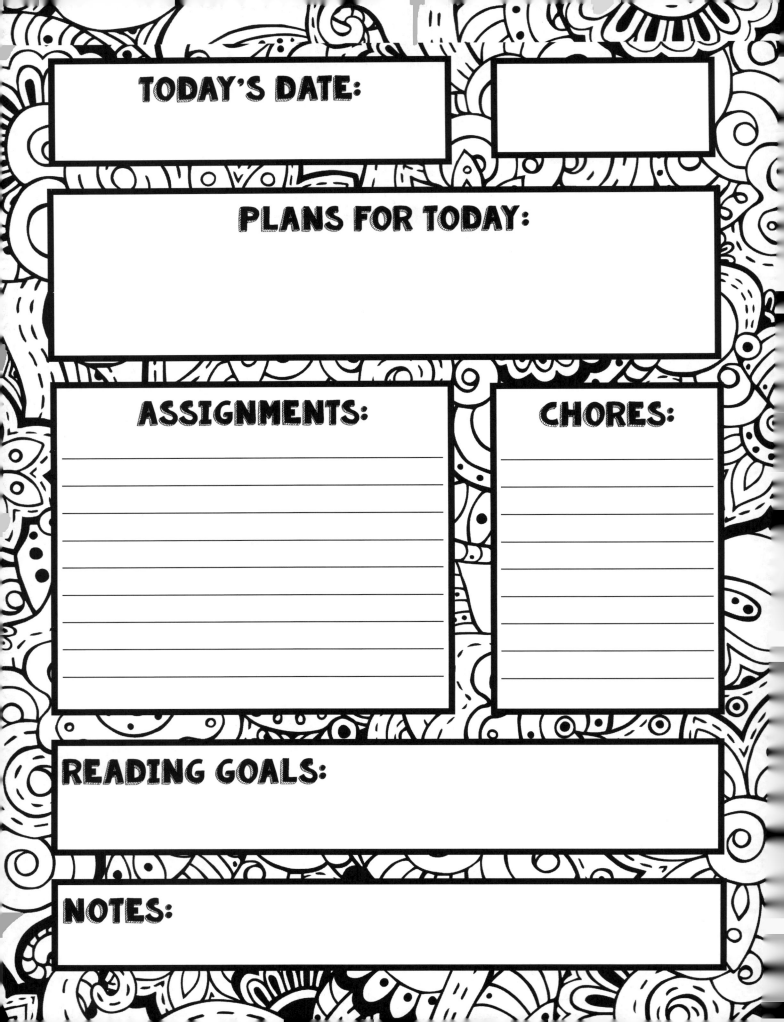

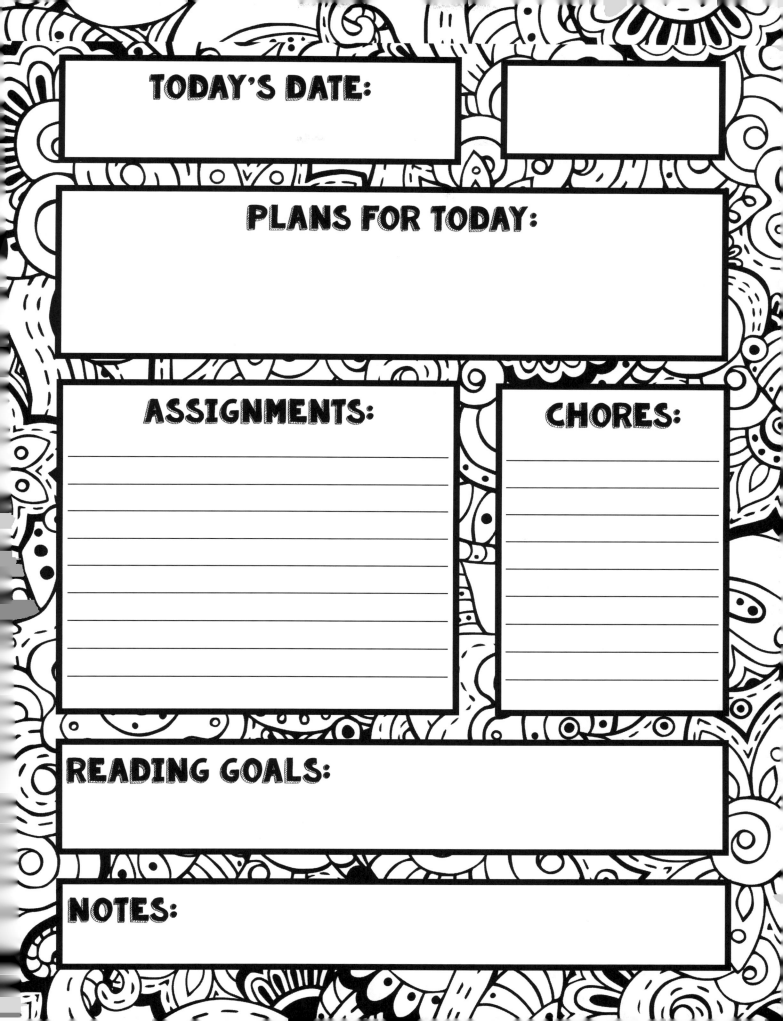

Plans & Perspective

"The home is the first and most effective place to learn the lessons of life: truth, honor, virtue, self control, the value of education, honest work, and the purpose and privilege of life." -McKay

My True Priorities

Long Term Goals

I Am Thankful For...

Checklist

Remember...

_____
_____
_____
_____
_____

180 Day Homeschool Planner & Organizer

Copyright Information

This Journal is for home and family use only. You may make copies of these materials for only the people in your household.

All other uses of this material must be permitted in writing by the Thinking Tree LLC. It is a violation of copyright law to distribute the electronic files or make copies for your friends, associates or students without our permission.

For information on using these materials for businesses, co-ops, summer camps, day camps, daycare, afterschool program, churches, or schools please contact us for licensing.

Contact Us:

The Thinking Tree LLC
617 N. Swope St. Greenfield, IN 46140. United States
317.622.8852 PHONE (Dial +1 outside of the USA) 267.712.7889 FAX

Do-It-Yourself Homeschooling
www.DyslexiaGames.com

jbrown@DyslexiaGames.com

Made in the USA
Lexington, KY
17 March 2017